DANIEL

THE IGNATIUS CATHOLIC STUDY BIBLE

REVISED STANDARD VERSION
SECOND CATHOLIC EDITION

DANIEL

With Introduction, Commentary, and Notes

by

Scott Hahn and Curtis Mitch

and

with Study Questions by

Dennis Walters

IGNATIUS PRESS SAN FRANCISCO

Published with ecclesiastical approval

Original RSV Bible text:
Nihil Obstat: Thomas Hanlon, S.T.L., L.S.S., Ph.L.
Imprimatur: +Peter W. Bartholome, D.D.
Bishop of Saint Cloud, Minnesota
May 11, 1966

Introduction, commentaries, and notes:
Nihil obstat: Rev. Msgr. J. Warren Holleran, S.T.D.
Imprimatur: +Most Reverend Salvatore J. Cordileone
Archbishop of San Francisco
July 15, 2013

The *nihil obstat* and *imprimatur* are official declarations that a book or pamphlet is free of doctrinal or moral error. No implication is contained therein that those who have granted the *nihil obstat* and *imprimatur* agree with the contents, opinions, or statements expressed.

Second Catholic Edition approved by the
National Council of the Churches of Christ in the USA

Cover art: HIP/Art Resource, New York

Cover design by Riz Boncan Marsella

Published by Ignatius Press in 2013

CONTENTS

INTRODUCTION TO
THE IGNATIUS CATHOLIC STUDY BIBLE
by Scott Hahn, Ph.D.

You are approaching the "word of God". This is the title Christians most commonly give to the Bible, and the expression is rich in meaning. It is also the title given to the Second Person of the Blessed Trinity, God the Son. For Jesus Christ became flesh for our salvation, and "the name by which he is called is The Word of God" (Rev 19:13; cf. Jn 1:14).

The word of God is Scripture. The Word of God is Jesus. This close association between God's *written* word and his *eternal* Word is intentional and has been the custom of the Church since the first generation. "All Sacred Scripture is but one book, and this one book is Christ, 'because all divine Scripture speaks of Christ, and all divine Scripture is fulfilled in Christ'[1]" (CCC 134). This does not mean that the Scriptures are divine in the same way that Jesus is divine. They are, rather, divinely inspired and, as such, are unique in world literature, just as the Incarnation of the eternal Word is unique in human history.

Yet we can say that the inspired word resembles the incarnate Word in several important ways. Jesus Christ is the Word of God incarnate. In his humanity, he is like us in all things, except for sin. As a work of man, the Bible is like any other book, except without error. Both Christ and Scripture, says the Second Vatican Council, are given "for the sake of salvation" (*Dei Verbum* 11), and both give us God's definitive revelation of himself. We cannot, therefore, conceive of one without the other: the Bible without Jesus, or Jesus without the Bible. Each is the interpretive key to the other. And because Christ is the subject of all the Scriptures, St. Jerome insists, "Ignorance of the Scriptures is ignorance of Christ"[2] (CCC 133).

When we approach the Bible, then, we approach Jesus, the Word of God; and in order to encounter Jesus, we must approach him in a prayerful study of the inspired word of God, the Sacred Scriptures.

Inspiration and Inerrancy The Catholic Church makes mighty claims for the Bible, and our acceptance of those claims is essential if we are to read the Scriptures and apply them to our lives as the Church intends. So it is not enough merely to nod at words like "inspired", "unique", or "inerrant". We have to understand what the Church means by these terms, and we have to make that understanding our

own. After all, what we believe about the Bible will inevitably influence the way we read the Bible. The way we read the Bible, in turn, will determine what we "get out" of its sacred pages.

These principles hold true no matter what we read: a news report, a search warrant, an advertisement, a paycheck, a doctor's prescription, an eviction notice. How (or whether) we read these things depends largely upon our preconceived notions about the reliability and authority of their sources—and the potential they have for affecting our lives. In some cases, to misunderstand a document's authority can lead to dire consequences. In others, it can keep us from enjoying rewards that are rightfully ours. In the case of the Bible, both the rewards and the consequences involved take on an ultimate value.

What does the Church mean, then, when she affirms the words of St. Paul: "All Scripture is inspired by God" (2 Tim 3:16)? Since the term "inspired" in this passage could be translated "God-breathed", it follows that God breathed forth his word in the Scriptures as you and I breathe forth air when we speak. This means that God is the primary author of the Bible. He certainly employed human authors in this task as well, but he did not merely assist them while they wrote or subsequently approve what they had written. God the Holy Spirit is the *principal* author of Scripture, while the human writers are *instrumental* authors. These human authors freely wrote everything, and only those things, that God wanted: the word of God in the very words of God. This miracle of dual authorship extends to the whole of Scripture, and to every one of its parts, so that whatever the human authors affirm, God likewise affirms through their words.

The principle of biblical inerrancy follows logically from this principle of divine authorship. After all, God cannot lie, and he cannot make mistakes. Since the Bible is divinely inspired, it must be without error in everything that its divine and human authors affirm to be true. This means that biblical inerrancy is a mystery even broader in scope than infallibility, which guarantees for us that the Church will always teach the truth concerning faith and morals. Of course the mantle of inerrancy likewise covers faith and morals, but it extends even farther to ensure that all the facts and events of salvation history are accurately presented for us in the Scriptures. Inerrancy is our guarantee that the words and deeds of God found in the Bible are unified and true,

---

[1] Hugh of St. Victor, *De arca Noe* 2, 8: PL 176, 642: cf. ibid. 2, 9: PL 176, 642–43.
[2] *DV* 25; cf. Phil 3:8 and St. Jerome, *Commentariorum in Isaiam libri xviii*, prol.: PL 24, 17b.

declaring with one voice the wonders of his saving love.

The guarantee of inerrancy does not mean, however, that the Bible is an all-purpose encyclopedia of information covering every field of study. The Bible is not, for example, a textbook in the empirical sciences, and it should not be treated as one. When biblical authors relate facts of the natural order, we can be sure they are speaking in a purely descriptive and "phenomenological" way, according to the way things appeared to their senses.

Biblical Authority Implicit in these doctrines is God's desire to make himself known to the world and to enter a loving relationship with every man, woman, and child he has created. God gave us the Scriptures not just to inform or motivate us; more than anything he wants to save us. This higher purpose underlies every page of the Bible, indeed every word of it.

In order to reveal himself, God used what theologians call "accommodation". Sometimes the Lord stoops down to communicate by "condescension"— that is, he speaks as humans speak, as if he had the same passions and weakness that we do (for example, God says he was "sorry" that he made man in Genesis 6:6). Other times he communicates by "elevation"—that is, by endowing human words with divine power (for example, through the Prophets). The numerous examples of divine accommodation in the Bible are an expression of God's wise and fatherly ways. For a sensitive father can speak with his children either by condescension, as in baby talk, or by elevation, by bringing a child's understanding up to a more mature level.

God's word is thus saving, fatherly, and personal. Because it speaks directly to us, we must never be indifferent to its content; after all, the word of God is at once the object, cause, and support of our faith. It is, in fact, a test of our faith, since we see in the Scriptures only what faith disposes us to see. If we believe what the Church believes, we will see in Scripture the saving, inerrant, and divinely authored revelation of the Father. If we believe otherwise, we see another book altogether.

This test applies not only to rank-and-file believers but also to the Church's theologians and hierarchy, and even the Magisterium. Vatican II has stressed in recent times that Scripture must be "the soul of sacred theology" (*Dei Verbum* 24). As Joseph Cardinal Ratzinger, Pope Emeritus Benedict XVI echoed this powerful teaching with his own, insisting that, "The *normative theologians* are the authors of Holy Scripture" (emphasis added). He reminded us that Scripture and the Church's dogmatic teaching are tied tightly together, to the point of being inseparable: "Dogma is by definition nothing other than an interpretation of Scripture." The defined dogmas of our faith, then, encapsulate the Church's infallible interpretation of Scripture, and theology is a further reflection upon that work.

The Senses of Scripture Because the Bible has both divine and human authors, we are required to master a different sort of reading than we are used to. First, we must read Scripture according to its *literal* sense, as we read any other human literature. At this initial stage, we strive to discover the meaning of the words and expressions used by the biblical writers as they were understood in their original setting and by their original recipients. This means, among other things, that we do not interpret everything we read "literalistically", as though Scripture never speaks in a figurative or symbolic way (it often does!). Rather, we read it according to the rules that govern its different literary forms of writing, depending on whether we are reading a narrative, a poem, a letter, a parable, or an apocalyptic vision. The Church calls us to read the divine books in this way to ensure that we understand what the human authors were laboring to explain to God's people.

The literal sense, however, is not the only sense of Scripture, since we interpret its sacred pages according to the *spiritual* senses as well. In this way, we search out what the Holy Spirit is trying to tell us, beyond even what the human authors have consciously asserted. Whereas the literal sense of Scripture describes a historical reality—a fact, precept, or event—the spiritual senses disclose deeper mysteries revealed through the historical realities. What the soul is to the body, the spiritual senses are to the literal. You can distinguish them; but if you try to separate them, death immediately follows. St. Paul was the first to insist upon this and warn of its consequences: "God ... has qualified us to be ministers of a new covenant, not in a written code but in the Spirit; for the written code kills, but the Spirit gives life" (2 Cor 3:5–6).

Catholic tradition recognizes three spiritual senses that stand upon the foundation of the literal sense of Scripture (see CCC 115). (**1**) The first is the *allegorical* sense, which unveils the spiritual and prophetic meaning of biblical history. Allegorical interpretations thus reveal how persons, events, and institutions of Scripture can point beyond themselves toward greater mysteries yet to come (OT) or display the fruits of mysteries already revealed (NT). Christians have often read the Old Testament in this way to discover how the mystery of Christ in the New Covenant was once hidden in the Old and how the full significance of the Old Covenant was finally made manifest in the New. Allegorical significance is likewise latent in the New Testament, especially in the life and deeds of Jesus recorded in the Gospels. Because Christ is the Head of the Church and the source of her spiritual life, what was accomplished in Christ the Head during his earthly life prefigures what he continually produces in his members through grace. The allegorical sense builds up the virtue of faith. (**2**) The second is the *tropological* or *moral* sense, which reveals how the actions of God's people in the Old Testament and the life of Jesus in the New Testament prompt us to form virtuous habits in our own lives. It therefore draws from Scripture warnings against sin and vice as well as inspirations to pursue holiness and purity. The moral sense is intended to build up the virtue of charity. (**3**) The third is the *anagogical* sense, which points upward to heavenly glory. It shows us how countless events in the Bible prefigure our final union with God in eternity and how things that are "seen" on earth are figures of things "unseen" in heaven. Because the anagogical sense leads us to contemplate our destiny, it is meant to build up the virtue of hope. Together with the literal sense, then, these spiritual senses draw out the fullness of what God wants to give us through his Word and as such comprise what ancient tradition has called the "full sense" of Sacred Scripture.

All of this means that the deeds and events of the Bible are charged with meaning beyond what is immediately apparent to the reader. In essence, that meaning is Jesus Christ and the salvation he died to give us. This is especially true of the books of the New Testament, which proclaim Jesus explicitly; but it is also true of the Old Testament, which speaks of Jesus in more hidden and symbolic ways. The human authors of the Old Testament told us as much as they were able, but they could not clearly discern the shape of all future events standing at such a distance. It is the Bible's divine Author, the Holy Spirit, who could and did foretell the saving work of Christ, from the first page of the Book of Genesis onward.

The New Testament did not, therefore, abolish the Old. Rather, the New fulfilled the Old, and in doing so, it lifted the veil that kept hidden the face of the Lord's bride. Once the veil is removed, we suddenly see the world of the Old Covenant charged with grandeur. Water, fire, clouds, gardens, trees, hills, doves, lambs—all of these things are memorable details in the history and poetry of Israel. But now, seen in the light of Jesus Christ, they are much more. For the Christian with eyes to see, water symbolizes the saving power of Baptism; fire, the Holy Spirit; the spotless lamb, Christ crucified; Jerusalem, the city of heavenly glory.

The spiritual reading of Scripture is nothing new. Indeed, the very first Christians read the Bible this way. St. Paul describes Adam as a "type" that prefigured Jesus Christ (Rom 5:14). A "type" is a real person, place, thing, or event in the Old Testament that foreshadows something greater in the New. From this term we get the word "typology", referring to the study of how the Old Testament prefigures Christ (CCC 128–30). Elsewhere St. Paul draws deeper meanings out of the story of Abraham's sons, declaring, "This is an allegory" (Gal 4:24). He is not suggesting that these events of the distant past never really happened; he is saying that

the events both happened *and* signified something more glorious yet to come.

The New Testament later describes the Tabernacle of ancient Israel as "a copy and shadow of the heavenly sanctuary" (Heb 8:5) and the Mosaic Law as a "shadow of the good things to come" (Heb 10:1). St. Peter, in turn, notes that Noah and his family were "saved through water" in a way that "corresponds" to sacramental Baptism, which "now saves you" (1 Pet 3:20–21). It is interesting to note that the expression translated as "corresponds" in this verse is a Greek term that denotes the fulfillment or counterpart of an ancient "type".

We need not look to the apostles, however, to justify a spiritual reading of the Bible. After all, Jesus himself read the Old Testament this way. He referred to Jonah (Mt 12:39), Solomon (Mt 12:42), the temple (Jn 2:19), and the brazen serpent (Jn 3:14) as "signs" that pointed forward to him. We see in Luke's Gospel, as Christ comforted the disciples on the road to Emmaus, that "beginning with Moses and all the prophets, he interpreted to them in all the Scriptures the things concerning himself" (Lk 24:27). It was precisely this extensive spiritual interpretation of the Old Testament that made such an impact on these once-discouraged travelers, causing their hearts to "burn" within them (Lk 24:32).

Criteria for Biblical Interpretation We, too, must learn to discern the "full sense" of Scripture as it includes both the literal and spiritual senses together. Still, this does not mean we should "read into" the Bible meanings that are not really there. Spiritual exegesis is not an unrestrained flight of the imagination. Rather, it is a sacred science that proceeds according to certain principles and stands accountable to sacred tradition, the Magisterium, and the wider community of biblical interpreters (both living and deceased).

In searching out the full sense of a text, we should always avoid the extreme tendency to "over-spiritualize" in a way that minimizes or denies the Bible's literal truth. St. Thomas Aquinas was well aware of this danger and asserted that "all other senses of Sacred Scripture are based on the literal" (*STh* I, 1, 10, *ad* 1, quoted in CCC 116). On the other hand, we should never confine the meaning of a text to the literal, intended sense of its human author, as if the divine Author did not intend the passage to be read in the light of Christ's coming.

Fortunately the Church has given us guidelines in our study of Scripture. The divine authorship of the Bible calls us to read it "in the sacred spirit in which it was written" (*Dei Verbum* 12). Vatican II outlines this teaching in a practical way by directing us to read the Scriptures according to three specific criteria:

1. We must "[b]e especially attentive 'to the content and unity of the whole Scripture'" (CCC 112).

2. We must "[r]ead the Scripture within 'the living Tradition of the whole Church'" (CCC 113).

3. We must "[b]e attentive to the analogy of faith" (CCC 114; cf. Rom 12:6).

These criteria protect us from many of the dangers that ensnare readers of the Bible, from the newest inquirer to the most prestigious scholar. Reading Scripture out of context is one such pitfall, and probably the one most difficult to avoid. A memorable cartoon from the 1950s shows a young man poring over the pages of the Bible. He says to his sister: "Don't bother me now; I'm trying to find a Scripture verse to back up one of my preconceived notions." No doubt a biblical text pried from its context can be twisted to say something very different from what its author actually intended.

The Church's criteria guide us here by defining what constitutes the authentic "context" of a given biblical passage. The first criterion directs us to the literary context of every verse, including not only the words and paragraphs that surround it, but also the entire corpus of the biblical author's writings and, indeed, the span of the entire Bible. The *complete* literary context of any Scripture verse includes every text from Genesis to Revelation—because the Bible is a unified book, not just a library of different books. When the Church canonized the Book of Revelation, for example, she recognized it to be incomprehensible apart from the wider context of the entire Bible.

The second criterion places the Bible firmly within the context of a community that treasures a "living tradition". That community is the People of God down through the ages. Christians lived out their faith for well over a millennium before the printing press was invented. For centuries, few believers owned copies of the Gospels, and few people could read anyway. Yet they absorbed the gospel—through the sermons of their bishops and clergy, through prayer and meditation, through Christian art, through liturgical celebrations, and through oral tradition. These were expressions of the one "living tradition", a culture of living faith that stretches from ancient Israel to the contemporary Church. For the early Christians, the gospel could not be understood apart from that tradition. So it is with us. Reverence for the Church's tradition is what protects us from any sort of chronological or cultural provincialism, such as scholarly fads that arise and carry away a generation of interpreters before being dismissed by the next generation.

The third criterion places scriptural texts within the framework of faith. If we believe that the Scriptures are divinely inspired, we must also believe them to be internally coherent and consistent with all the doctrines that Christians believe. Remember, the Church's dogmas (such as the Real Presence, the papacy, the Immaculate Conception) are not something *added* to Scripture; rather, they are the Church's infallible interpretation *of* Scripture.

Using This Study Guide This volume is designed to lead the reader through Scripture according to the Church's guidelines—faithful to the canon, to the tradition, and to the creeds. The Church's interpretive principles have thus shaped the component parts of this book, and they are designed to make the reader's study as effective and rewarding as possible.

Introductions: We have introduced the biblical book with an essay covering issues such as authorship, date of composition, purpose, and leading themes. This background information will assist readers to approach and understand the text on its own terms.

Annotations: The basic notes at the bottom of every page help the user to read the Scriptures with understanding. They by no means exhaust the meaning of the sacred text but provide background material to help the reader make sense of what he reads. Often these notes make explicit what the sacred writers assumed or held to be implicit. They also provide a great deal of historical, cultural, geographical, and theological information pertinent to the inspired narratives—information that can help the reader bridge the distance between the biblical world and his own.

Cross-References: Between the biblical text at the top of each page and the annotations at the bottom, numerous references are listed to point readers to other scriptural passages related to the one being studied. This follow-up is an essential part of any serious study. It is also an excellent way to discover how the content of Scripture "hangs together" in a providential unity. Along with biblical cross-references, the annotations refer to select paragraphs from the *Catechism of the Catholic Church*. These are not doctrinal "proof texts" but are designed to help the reader interpret the Bible in accordance with the mind of the Church. The Catechism references listed either handle the biblical text directly or treat a broader doctrinal theme that sheds significant light on that text.

Topical Essays, Word Studies, Charts: These features bring readers to a deeper understanding of select details. The *topical essays* take up major themes and explain them more thoroughly and theologically than the annotations, often relating them to the doctrines of the Church. Occasionally the annotations are supplemented by *word studies* that put readers in touch with the ancient languages of Scripture. These should help readers to understand better and appreciate the inspired terminology that runs throughout the sacred books. Also included are various *charts* that summarize biblical information "at a glance".

Icon Annotations: Three distinctive icons are interspersed throughout the annotations, each one corresponding to one of the Church's three criteria for biblical interpretation. Bullets indicate the passage or passages to which these icons apply.

Notes marked by the book icon relate to the "content and unity" of Scripture, showing how particular passages of the Old Testament illuminate the mysteries of the New. Much of the information in these notes explains the original context of the citations and indicates how and why this has a direct bearing on Christ or the Church. Through these notes, the reader can develop a sensitivity to the beauty and unity of God's saving plan as it stretches across both Testaments.

Notes marked by the dove icon examine particular passages in light of the Church's "living tradition". Because the Holy Spirit both guides the Magisterium and inspires the spiritual senses of Scripture, these annotations supply information along both of these lines. On the one hand, they refer to the Church's doctrinal teaching as presented by various popes, creeds, and ecumenical councils; on the other, they draw from (and paraphrase) the spiritual interpretations of various Fathers, Doctors, and saints.

Notes marked by the keys icon pertain to the "analogy of faith". Here we spell out how the mysteries of our faith "unlock" and explain one another. This type of comparison between Christian beliefs displays the coherence and unity of defined dogmas, which are the Church's infallible interpretations of Scripture.

Putting It All in Perspective Perhaps the most important context of all we have saved for last:

the interior life of the individual reader. What we get out of the Bible will largely depend on how we approach the Bible. Unless we are living a sustained and disciplined life of prayer, we will never have the reverence, the profound humility, or the grace we need to see the Scriptures for what they really are.

You are approaching the "word of God". But for thousands of years, since before he knit you in your mother's womb, the Word of God has been approaching you.

One Final Note. The volume you hold in your hands is only a small part of a much larger work still in production. Study helps similar to those printed in this booklet are being prepared for *all* the books of the Bible and will appear gradually as they are finished. Our ultimate goal is to publish a single, one-volume Study Bible that will include the entire text of Scripture, along with all the annotations, charts, cross-references, maps, and other features found in the following pages. Individual booklets will be published in the meantime, with the hope that God's people can begin to benefit from this labor before its full completion.

We have included a long list of Study Questions in the back to make this format as useful as possible, not only for individual study, but for group settings and discussions as well. The questions are designed to help readers both "understand" the Bible and "apply" it to their lives. We pray that God will make use of our efforts and yours to help renew the face of the earth! «

INTRODUCTION TO DANIEL

Author and Date The long-standing position of Jewish and Christian tradition holds that the Book of Daniel was written by the prophet Daniel himself in the sixth century B.C. This view was mainly unquestioned until modern times, which have witnessed vigorous challenges to the Danielic authorship and sixth-century dating of the book along with new proposals about its origin and time of composition. Both positions have defenders today.

(1) *Danielic authorship, sixth-century date.* Some scholars hold that Daniel authored the book near the end of his ministry, around 535 B.C. In addition to claiming the support of Jewish and Christian theologians over the centuries, advocates contend that Daniel is the candidate who best fits the profile of the author and his time period that emerges from the internal data of the book. Evidence said to support this position includes the following: (a) Daniel 1–6 appears to have been written by someone knowledgeable about political and exilic conditions in Babylonia and Persia in the sixth century B.C. Even incidental details in these narratives have been verified as accurate by Near Eastern sources outside the Bible (see notes on 1:1; 5:1; 6:7). Proponents admit that historical difficulties remain in these early chapters; nevertheless, they insist that enough has been shown to line up with non-biblical evidence to conclude that the stories about Daniel and his friends rest on genuine historical memories, presumably from someone close to the events. Daniel meets this criterion as well or better than any, since he held government positions in both the Babylonian and Persian kingdoms (see 2:48; 6:1–2). (b) The Aramaic in the central section of the book, running from 2:4b to 7:28, is convincingly classified as Imperial or Official Aramaic, which was the international language of diplomacy and commerce in the Near East from ca. 700 to 300 B.C. Allowing for some updating in spelling, due to phonetic shifts that occurred over time in the spoken language, it has been argued that the Aramaic in Daniel stands closer to that used in the Babylonian and early Persian periods (sixth and fifth centuries B.C.) than that used in the late Persian and Hellenistic periods (fourth, third, and second centuries B.C.). This does not prove that Daniel was the author; however, it coheres with the fact that Daniel was one of the few Jewish exiles in Babylon handpicked to be educated in Aramaic (called "the letters and language of the Chaldeans" in 1:4). (c) The vision reports in Daniel 7–12 are all written in the first person (I, me, my), with the name of the visionary given as "Daniel"

(7:2; 8:1; 9:2; 10:1, etc.). This gives the impression that these chapters are excerpts drawn directly from Daniel's personal memoirs. (d) The author claims that the visions in chapters 7–12 anticipate a fulfillment that lies beyond his lifetime (8:26; 10:14; 12:5–13). On the one hand, this information is too generic to insist that the Book of Daniel must have appeared in the sixth century B.C. and no other. Even so, it seems to count against the modern position, which posits that a writer living centuries after Daniel composed the book as a prophetic interpretation of recent events rather than a prophetic prediction of future events.

(2) *Non-Danielic authorship, second-century date.* Most modern scholars argue that the book was written under the name "Daniel" by an unknown Jewish author in the second century B.C., perhaps around 164. Proponents typically view the book as a response to the assault on Palestinian Judaism by the Seleucid ruler Antiochus IV Epiphanes, a crisis that reached its height between 167 and 164 B.C. A number of observations form the basis of this position: (a) Several historical notations in Daniel 1–6 conflict with reports of the same time period given by classical and Near Eastern sources. If the writer was confused about his facts, then scholars reason that these stories are not likely to have come from someone who witnessed or heard about them firsthand. It is easier to account for historical blunders if the author was writing long after the events he describes. (b) The visions in Daniel 11 that concern Hellenistic history leading up to the death of Antiochus are quite accurate. This leads many to suggest that the author of Daniel must have lived in the days of Antiochus and was writing about events of recent history, which he made look like prophecy by expressing them in apocalyptic language. Indeed, the technique of composing "prophecies after the fact" (known in Latin as *vaticinia ex eventu*), and doing so in the name of a revered figure from Israel's past (known as "pseudepigraphy"), is said to be a constitutive feature of Jewish apocalyptic writings that appeared between roughly 300 B.C. and A.D. 300. (c) In the arrangement of the Hebrew Bible, the Book of Daniel is grouped, not with the Prophets, but among a class of books known as the Writings. This suggests to some that Daniel must have been written later than the canonization of the prophetical books around the fifth century B.C. Moreover, the Book of Sirach mentions Isaiah, Jeremiah, and Ezekiel by name and refers collectively to the Twelve Minor Prophets but never mentions Daniel (Sir 48:20; 49:6–10). The implication

often drawn is that Daniel postdates, not only the canonization of the Prophets, but even the composition of Sirach, which appeared in Hebrew around 180 B.C. (d) The religious outlook of the author is said to fall within a range of Jewish theological opinions that had currency in the second century B.C. Certain scholars identify the writer as one of the *Ḥasidim*, or loyal observers of Torah (called "Hasideans" in 1 Mac 2:42 and 2 Mac 14:6), some of whom joined forces with the Maccabees in fighting a guerilla war against Antiochus IV. Others maintain that the book was authored by one of the *Maskilim*, a group of teachers (called "wise" in Dan 11:33, 35; 12:3) who advocated nonviolent resistance to the Seleucid persecution of Judaism.

Establishing the authorship and date of the Book of Daniel is a matter too complex to admit of simple answers. Complicating factors are many and varied, and virtually every argument claimed in support of the traditional and modern positions has been contested. Regarding the traditional view, it may be said that insistence on Daniel's authorship of the entire book is not demanded by the claims of the text, since the first-person narration in Daniel 7–12 (I, me, my) is balanced by third-person narration throughout the rest of the book (Daniel, he, his). This could well suggest that someone other than Daniel had a hand in compiling the book, even if Daniel or his personal writings served as a primary source of information. Likewise, the linguistic evidence is capable of different interpretations, so the argument for a sixth-century date on the basis of Daniel's Aramaic is more suggestive than conclusive. With respect to the modern argument against the traditional view, all scholars recognize that Daniel 1–6 presents the reader with some formidable historical conundrums. Nevertheless, reasonable solutions to these problems have been proposed by advocates of the traditional view, and these should not be dismissed out of hand on the all-too-easy supposition that the inspired author had a deficient historical knowledge or that he deemed it acceptable to fabricate stories or characters in the interests of his theological agenda. Likewise, the accurate prediction of events after the lifetime of Daniel must not be counted as evidence against the antiquity or authenticity of the visions, as though it offends reason to hold that God knows the future and is able to reveal it in detail to his prophets. Historical research runs afoul when conducted with a presuppositional bias against the possibility of inspired foreknowledge. Lastly, Daniel's placement among the Writings of the Hebrew Bible and not the Prophets tells us more about the development of the biblical canon in rabbinic Judaism than about the date when Daniel first appeared in writing. Some have even hypothesized that rabbinical authorities moved Daniel from the Prophets to the Writings after the failure of the Second Jewish Revolt against Rome (A.D. 135). The evidence for this is not conclusive, but sources written prior to the Revolt are consistent in showing that Palestinian Jews, including Jesus, considered Daniel a "prophet" (Mt 24:15; 4QFlor 2, 3; Josephus, *Antiquities* 10, 249).

Account must also be taken of the deuterocanonical sections of Daniel that appear in the Greek translations of the book (*3:1–68* in *italics*; 13:1–64; 14:1–42). These parts of the book are accepted as inspired and canonical by the Catholic Church, yet they are not found in any surviving Hebrew-Aramaic versions of the book. Many regard these extra materials as independent traditions added by a different author writing in Greek, perhaps near the end of the second century B.C. This is possible, although some evidence suggests that the alleged Greek insertions are translations made from Semitic originals. To date, however, there is no surviving proof that a Hebrew or Aramaic version of all fourteen chapters of Daniel circulated as a single work.

In the end, a modified form of the traditional view seems to satisfy the greatest amount of evidence and require the least amount of unsupported speculation. This is the position that the Book of Daniel had its origin in the sixth century B.C., that its testimony has links with the prophet Daniel himself, but that the canonical form of the book postdates the lifetime of Daniel. Still, the majority view maintains that the Book of Daniel is mainly a product of the second century B.C., even if the initial stories about Daniel in chapters 1–6 circulated as oral (or written) tradition before an unknown Jewish author worked them into the book we have today.

Title The book takes its name from its principal hero, Daniel, who lived as a Jewish exile and civil servant in Babylon. His name in Hebrew, *Daniy'el*, means "God is my Judge." In the Hebrew canon, Daniel stands between Esther and Ezra in the third division of books called the Writings. In the Greek Septuagint, the book is likewise entitled *Daniēl* but is grouped instead with the Major Prophets and is placed either before or after Ezekiel. The Latin Vulgate follows the Greek order of books but supplies the fuller heading *Prophetia Danielis*, "The Prophecy of Daniel".

Structure The canonical form of Daniel has three principal divisions. (**1**) Chapters 1–6 are a collection of six "court tales" about Daniel and his friends working as royal ministers in Babylon. Lessons about fidelity in the midst of trial and a firm belief that God will vindicate his faithful servants stand out prominently. These chapters exhibit notable similarities with the Book of Esther and with the Joseph stories of the Book of Genesis. (**2**) Chapters 7–12 form a collection of "apocalyptic visions" that Daniel received in four installments. These visual prophecies claim to reveal the future course of Near Eastern politics in relation to God's plan for the unfolding of salvation history. (**3**) Chapters 13–14 form an appendix that showcases Daniel's wisdom in prosecuting injustice and exposing the folly of idolatry.

Literary Background The Book of Daniel survives as a trilingual composition written in Hebrew, Aramaic, and Greek. It begins in Hebrew (1:1—2:4a), switches to Aramaic for several chapters (2:4b—7:28), and then reverts back to Hebrew for several more chapters (8:1—12:13). Its Greek portions include the Prayer of Azariah (*3:1–27* in *italics*), the Song of the Three Young Men (*3:28–68* in *italics*), and three concluding stories, Susanna (13:1–64) and Bel and the Dragon (14:1–42). For the most part, the Greek text endorsed by Christian tradition is not the Septuagint version of Daniel (LXX) but a translation associated with a figure from the second century A.D. named Theodotian (abbreviated Θ).

In terms of literary genre, the Book of Daniel is usually classified as "apocalyptic literature". Apocalyptic is a form of prophecy that depicts the future through symbolic images and story lines. This type of literature, which flourished in Jewish and then Christian circles between ca. 300 B.C. and A.D. 300, consists of divine revelations about the meaning and direction of history given to select individuals, often through the mediation of angels. Distinctive of the apocalyptic genre is its graphic and sometimes bizarre use of cosmic and animal symbolism to represent heavenly and historical realities. Apocalyptic literature is also a type of crisis literature that arises out of times of community affliction, when God's people are made to endure religious or political oppression. Its purpose is to encourage the downtrodden with the hope that God will intervene to right the wrongs of the world and to reward the faithful for their perseverance. Early specimens of apocalyptic prophecy can be found, for example, in Isaiah 24–27 and Zechariah 9–14, while more developed examples of Jewish apocalyptic include such non-biblical works as *1 Enoch*, *4 Ezra*, and *2 Baruch*. The clearest example of a Christian apocalypse is the Book of Revelation, which relies heavily on Daniel for several of its images, themes, and expressions.

Themes The Book of Daniel often strikes readers as fascinating and frustrating at the same time. Its stories entertain and encourage, yet its visions can seem impenetrably obscure and unedifying. A conflicting array of interpretations also abounds in the popular culture, sparking interest in some and a strong disinterest in others. Perhaps the main challenge in discovering the message of Daniel is to step back from its details to consider the big picture. Daniel is basically a book about *heroism* and *history* from the perspective of God and his Providence. These are not the only themes that have a place in the book; nevertheless, they underlie many of its symbols and subplots and may be considered a helpful starting point for reading the book with understanding.

(**1**) Stories about *heroism* dominate the prose accounts that stand at the beginning (chaps. 1–6) and end of Daniel (chaps. 13–14). The occasion for these is the Babylonian Exile, where the faith of Israel clashes with the idolatrous culture of the Gentiles. In this context, Jewish allegiance to Yahweh often leads the faithful into times of testing and trial. When the story begins, Daniel and his friends, for fear of defilement, decline the royal food allowance assigned to them. They instead eat only vegetables, and as a result the Lord rewards and prospers them for refusing to compromise their faith (1:3–21). Later on, Daniel's young friends Shadrach, Meshach, and Abednego defy the royal demand of Nebuchadnezzar to bow in reverence before an imposing idol. For this, they are cast into a fiery furnace, at which point the Lord sends an angel from heaven to protect them and to bring them out unharmed (3:1–30). Under a subsequent king, Daniel himself is forced to transgress a royal decree that would violate his commitment to Yahweh. Unwilling to forsake his daily prayers, he is condemned to the lions' den, only to experience God's deliverance from the mouths of the beasts (6:1–24). At the end of the book, Daniel takes proactive steps to expose the falsehoods of pagan religion, even destroying idols and unworthy objects of veneration (14:1–30). Once again, he is condemned to death in a pit of lions, only to be saved by the miraculous intervention of God (14:31–42). The story of Susanna, although not presenting a conflict between idolatry and Israelite belief, nevertheless continues the motif of trials in a land of exile, highlighting how entrusting oneself to the Lord can bring vindication and rescue from the schemes of the godless (13:1–64). Through circumstances such as these, the heroes (and heroine) of the Book of Daniel stand as witnesses to the power and greatness of Yahweh as the Protector of his people and the only true God over the world.

(**2**) Prophetic insights into *history* are found mainly in the book's dreams (chaps. 2, 7) and visions (chaps. 8–12). Central to the revelations contained in these chapters is the Lordship of Yahweh over the direction of world events. In this respect, Daniel's perspective is in line with the providentialist history of the Bible as a whole. This is the notion that God, far from being a mere spectator or absentee landlord, is directly involved in human events and steers the course of history to fulfill his saving plan. Scripture often makes this point with reference to Israel, but Daniel shows us that God also controls the fortunes of nations beyond Israel, including the great empires of the ancient Near East.

This is most obvious in chapters 2 and 7, where Nebuchadnezzar and Daniel both have dreams about the succession of political powers in the region. Just as the king sees a human image made of four metals, each representing a different Gentile empire (2:31–35), so the prophet sees the same sequence in terms of four beasts crawling up out of the sea (7:1–8). Scholars disagree on the identity of some of these kingdoms, but according to the dominant view of Christian tradition, the four kingdoms are Neo-Babylonia, Medo-Persia, Greece, and Rome—the succession of foreign governments that subjugated Israel in the exilic and postexilic periods of the OT. Each will play its part in the divine plan for history, but the main point of the message is that God will stand in triumph over the four empires by establishing his own kingdom in the world for all time (2:44–45; 7:13–27). Unlike these worldly powers, the Lord's kingdom will be everlasting and indestructible. His reign will be exercised through a figure who appears in Daniel as a "son of man" (7:13).

Chapter 9 likewise anticipates God's intervention in history, only this time from the vantage point of Israel. It is a message of hope in the face of prolonged suffering. Israel in Daniel's day had been forcibly exiled from Palestine because of sin. The prophet laments this catastrophe, which took place in the sixth century B.C., and when he prays for the restoration of God's people, he is told that Israel will have to remain humbled for another seventy weeks of years (= 490 years) before God's mercy and forgiveness are poured out in full measure (9:24). This will coincide historically with the arrival of the kingdom of God and its victory over the four empires. Thus, the Lord's own kingdom will come when, at the end of the seventy weeks of years, he makes atonement for sin and brings everlasting righteousness to his people. At this time, the world will witness the coming of an "anointed one" who will be "cut off" (9:26). The death of this messiah figure will result in the demise of Jerusalem and the decisive end of sanctuary worship in Israel (9:26–27).

Finally, despite the troubles that Daniel envisions for his people in the future, and even beyond the spiritual blessings that will come with the Lord's kingdom, the saints who persevere through tribulation can expect the eventual resurrection of their bodies and the inheritance of eternal life (12:1–2). Having shown themselves wise, they will shine "like the stars for ever and ever" (12:3). From the standpoint of God and his Providence, this is the goal of history in the most ultimate sense.

Christian Perspective Several times the New Testament makes reference to the Book of Daniel. In the Gospels, Jesus speaks of the mystery or secret of the kingdom of God that is disclosed through his ministry (Mk 4:11; cf. Mt 13:11). The link between "mystery" and "kingdom" suggests an allusion to this dual motif in Daniel's account of Nebuchadnezzar's dream (Dan 2:18–19, 27–28, 30, 44). The same background probably stands behind Paul's discussion of "mystery" as well, especially in Ephesians, where it refers to God's plan of salvation as it unfolds in history and extends to the Gentiles (Eph 1:9–10; 3:4–6). Related to this, Jesus not only calls himself the "Son of man" on numerous occasions but even links this title to Daniel's vision of the Son of man riding on the clouds of heaven (Mt 24:30; 26:64). And in his eschatological discourse, Jesus prophesies the profanation of the Jerusalem Temple by a "desolating sacrilege" (Mt 24:15), a cryptic expression based on Daniel's references to an "abomination that makes desolate" (Dan 11:31; 12:11). Finally, the Book of Revelation borrows a number of images (Rev 14:14; Dan 7:13), symbols (Rev 13:1–2; Dan 7:1–8), and phrases from Daniel (Rev 12:14; Dan 7:25). Part of the message of Revelation, and of the NT in general, is that Daniel's prophecies have come to fulfillment in Jesus Christ and his everlasting kingdom.

OUTLINE OF DANIEL

1. Daniel and His Three Friends (chaps. 1–6)
   A. Exiles at the Court of Babylon (1:1–21)
   B. The First Dream of Nebuchadnezzar (2:1–49)
   C. The Idol and the Fiery Furnace (3:1–30 plus *3:1–68* in *italics*).
   D. The Second Dream of Nebuchadnezzar (4:1–37)
   E. Belshazzar and the Writing on the Wall (5:1–30)
   F. Daniel and the Lions' Den (6:1–28)

2. Daniel and His Four Visions (chaps. 7–12)
   A. The Four Beasts and the Son of Man (7:1–28)
   B. The Ram and the He-Goat (8:1–27)
   C. The Prayer of Daniel and the Seventy Weeks (9:1–27)
   D. The Time of the End and the Resurrection (10:1—12:13)

3. Daniel the Wise and Clever (chaps. 13–14)
   A. The Story of Susanna (13:1–64)
   B. The Story of Bel and the Dragon (14:1–42)

THE BOOK OF

DANIEL

Four Young Israelites at the Babylonian Court

1 In the third year of the reign of Jehoi'akim king of Judah, Nebuchadnez'zar king of Babylon came to Jerusalem and besieged it. ²And the Lord gave Jehoi'akim king of Judah into his hand, with some of the vessels of the house of God; and he brought them to the land of Shi'nar, to the house of his god, and placed the vessels in the treasury of his god. ³Then the king commanded Ash'penaz, his chief eunuch, to bring some of the people of Israel, both of the royal family and of the nobility, ⁴youths without blemish, handsome and skilful in all wisdom, endowed with knowledge, understanding learning, and competent to serve in the king's palace, and to teach them the letters and language of the Chalde'ans. ⁵The king assigned them a daily portion of the rich food which the king ate, and of the wine which he drank. They were to be educated for three years, and at the end of that time they were to stand before the king. ⁶Among these were Daniel, Hanani'ah, Mish'a-el, and Azari'ah of the tribe of Judah. ⁷And the chief of the eunuchs gave them names: Daniel he called Belteshaz'zar, Hanani'ah he called Shad'rach, Mish'a-el he called Me'shach, and Azari'ah he called Abed'nego.

8 But Daniel resolved that he would not defile himself* with the king's rich food, or with the wine which he drank; therefore he asked the chief

---

1:1–7 The setting of the book is the Babylonian Exile. Daniel was among the first captives from Judah deported to Babylon in 605 B.C., and he remained in the East until at least 537 B.C., the third year after Cyrus II of Persia conquered Babylon (10:1).

1:1 third year: 605 B.C., designated Jehoiakim's "fourth year" in Jer 46:2. Some regard this discrepancy of one year as problematic, along with the fact that historical sources do not otherwise attest to a Babylonian siege of Jerusalem at this time. Nevertheless, a plausible resolution may be reached on the basis of two considerations. (1) Two different systems of counting a king's reign were used in the Near East, one that included and one that excluded the accession year in the total years of his rule. This would account for the disparity of one year in dating the reign of Jehoiakim relative to the military exploits of Nebuchadnezzar. (2) Babylonian evidence indicates that Nebuchadnezzar, following his triumph over Egypt at the battle of Carchemish in the summer of 605, proceeded to march victoriously through Syria-Palestine. No explicit mention is made of an assault on Jerusalem, but it stands to reason that such a campaign would include a show of force in the Jewish

capital, since the king of Judah was a political vassal of Egypt appointed by Pharaoh Neco (2 Kings 23:34). **Jehoiakim:** King of Judah from 609 until 598 B.C. **Nebuchadnezzar:** Reigned from 605 until 562 B.C. as the mightiest king of the Neo-Babylonian empire. He deported thousands of Judeans as exiles to Babylon (2 Kings 24:10–17; 25:11) and eventually destroyed the Jerusalem Temple (2 Kings 25:8–10). **besieged:** Following this event in 605 B.C., the Bible knows of three subsequent incursions into Judea by Nebuchadnezzar: one in 601 (2 Kings 24:1–2), one in 597 (2 Kings 24:10–17), and one in 586 (2 Kings 25:8–12).

1:2 vessels: Nebuchadnezzar plunders the Jerusalem Temple and carries off vessels used for worship. During this first raid, the king confiscates only "some" of the vessels; years later he will seize "all" the furnishings of the Temple (2 Chron 36:18). **land of Shinar:** Babylonia on the lower Mesopotamian plain (Gen 10:10; 11:2). **the house of his god:** The temple of Marduk, also called Bel, the high god of the Neo-Babylonian pantheon (14:3). The transfer of sacred vessels from one temple to another introduces a theme of divine contest that develops throughout the book. At first, it appears the God of Israel has been conquered and despoiled by the chief deity of Babylon. But the very moment these vessels are defiled in honor of false gods, the kingdom of Babylon is overthrown (5:1–4). Time and again the book shows that Yahweh is the "Most High God" (4:2), the Sovereign Lord of creation and history (2:20–23, 47; 3:28–29; 4:34–37, etc.).

1:3 Ashpenaz: Headmaster at the government academy that trained future statesmen and civil servants.

1:4 teach them: Courtiers in Semitic kingdoms were educated to serve the king as scribes, lawyers, diplomats, archivists, translators, etc. **language of the Chaldeans:** Aramaic, the language of international affairs spoken and written throughout the Near East at this time.

1:7 gave them names: Daniel and his friends have names that incorporate the name of God (the Hebrew element is either 'el, meaning "God", or yah, which is short for "Yahweh"). Their new names, which mark them as servants of Nebuchadnezzar, make reference to the names of Babylonian deities ("Bel", "Aku", and "Nabu/Nego").

1:8 not defile himself: Daniel takes steps to avoid dietary defilement, the nature of which is unclear since the Torah does not regard "meat" or "wine" as generally unfit for Jewish consumption (10:3). Possible factors behind Daniel's decision include the following: (1) A few types of meat are declared

---

The book is composed of two distinct parts. In the first, there are stories about Daniel in the time of the Babylonian Empire; in the second, there are a number of apocalyptic visions ascribed to Daniel and foretelling the future. The stories of the first part may be based on original material dating from the time of Daniel but must have been written down later, as they betray an unfamiliarity with the history of the period. Likewise, the visions of the second part are predominantly concerned with the later Greek Empire and it is unlikely that they were composed before that time. Their literary form, too, corresponds to the apocalyptic style of literature common in the second century B.C. The Greek version has some portions not in the Hebrew or Aramaic and these are accepted as canonical by the Catholic Church. They are: The Prayer of Azariah and the Song of the Three Young Men (3:1–68); Susanna (chapter 13); Bel and the Dragon (chapter 14). In the rest of the book there are some parts written in Aramaic, thus suggesting a rather late date.

In the first part of the book, the main purpose is to exalt the God of Israel over the gods of the pagans through the experiences of the prophet Daniel. In the second part, the aim is equally to exalt the God of Israel, but this time it is done through a series of visions in which many prophecies are made—the chief of which is the seventy weeks of years until the coming of the Messiah (9:24). The author aims at sustaining the faith of the people of God during difficult times culminating in the persecution of Antiochus Epiphanes.

* 1:8, *would not defile himself:* When the Greek persecution broke out, the king tried to get the Jews to break their laws about food and drink, and such breaches of the law were taken to be apostasy; cf. 2 Mac 6:18—7:42.

of the eunuchs to allow him not to defile himself. [9]And God gave Daniel favor and compassion in the sight of the chief of the eunuchs; [10]and the chief of the eunuchs said to Daniel, "I fear lest my lord the king, who appointed your food and your drink, should see that you were in poorer condition than the youths who are of your own age. So you would endanger my head with the king." [11]Then Daniel said to the steward whom the chief of the eunuchs had appointed over Daniel, Hanani′ah, Mish′a-el, and Azari′ah; [12]"Test your servants for ten days; let us be given vegetables to eat and water to drink. [13]Then let our appearance and the appearance of the youths who eat the king's rich food be observed by you, and according to what you see deal with your servants." [14]So he listened to them in this matter, and tested them for ten days. [15]At the end of ten days it was seen that they were better in appearance and fatter in flesh than all the youths who ate the king's rich food. [16]So the steward took away their rich food and the wine they were to drink, and gave them vegetables.

17 As for these four youths, God gave them learning and skill in all letters and wisdom; and Daniel had understanding in all visions and dreams. [18]At the end of the time, when the king had commanded that they should be brought in, the chief of the eunuchs brought them in before Nebuchadnez′zar. [19]And the king spoke with them, and among them all none was found like Daniel, Hanani′ah, Mish′a-el, and Azari′ah; therefore they stood before the king. [20]And in every matter of wisdom and understanding concerning which the king inquired of them, he found them ten times better than all the magicians and enchanters that were in all his kingdom. [21]And Daniel continued until the first year of King Cyrus.

2 In the second year of the reign of Nebuchad-nez′zar, Nebuchadnezzar had dreams; and his spirit was troubled, and his sleep left him. [2]Then the king commanded that the magicians, the enchanters, the sorcerers, and the Chalde′ans be summoned, to tell the king his dreams. So they came in and stood before the king. [3]And the king said to them, "I had a dream, and my spirit is troubled to know the dream." [4]Then the Chalde′ans said to the king,[a] "O king, live for ever! Tell your servants the dream, and we will show the interpretation." [5]The king answered the Chalde′ans, "The word from me is sure: if you do not make known to me the dream and its interpretation, you shall be torn limb from limb, and your houses shall be laid in ruins. [6]But if you show the dream and its interpretation, you shall receive from me gifts and rewards and great honor. Therefore show me the dream and its interpretation." [7]They answered a second time, "Let the king tell his servants the dream, and we will show its interpretation." [8]The king answered,

---

unclean by the Law, e.g., the flesh of swine, horses, and various birds (Lev 11:1–47). (2) No meat is deemed suitable for eating unless it is carefully drained of blood (Lev 17:10–14). (3) Persons who professed a Nazarite vow refrained from wine (Num 6:1–4). (4) Gentiles of the ancient world often consecrated their foods to idols (1 Cor 8:7), with the result that abstinence from pagan foods became a hallmark of Jewish fidelity in biblical times (Tob 1:10–12; Jud 10:5; 12:1–2; 1 Mac 1:62–63; Rom 14:2, 21). Whatever issue(s) prompted his actions, it is clear that Daniel refuses to compromise his religious commitment to Yahweh at table.

1:12 ten days: A time of testing (Rev 2:10). Faithfulness to the Lord throughout this trial period makes Daniel and his friends "ten times" as wise as the sages of Babylon (1:20).

1:21 first year of King Cyrus: 539 B.C., the year Cyrus II of Persia conquered Babylon and seized control of its empire. His reign as king of Persia began two decades earlier in 559 B.C. Daniel must have been at least 70 years old when he entered the service of Cyrus II.

2:1–49 Daniel begins his career as wise man and courtier. Evidence outside the Bible confirms that foreigners could be promoted to high political office in the Neo-Babylonian government. • Daniel's rise to the royal court in Babylon recalls the story of Joseph's elevation to power in Egypt. In both cases, a Gentile king has mysterious dreams about the future (2:31–45; Gen 41:25–36) that trouble his spirit (2:1; Gen 41:8). After the king's court magicians fail to unravel the mystery (2:2–11; Gen 41:8), a Hebrew exile is brought forward to explain the symbolism of the dream (2:25; Gen 41:9–15), although he insists that God is the real interpreter of its meaning (2:27–30; Gen 41:16). Promotion of the Hebrew sage follows thereafter (2:48–49; Gen 41:37–44).

2:1 second year: 604 B.C., a date that appears to stand in tension with the chronological information given in 1:5 and 18, which requires three years to elapse before Daniel can stand before Nebuchadnezzar as a fully trained court sage. One possible reason for the difference is that the number was miscopied at an early stage in the scribal transmission of the book. A Greek papyrus dating to the second or third century A.D. reads "twelfth year". **dreams:** Often channels of divine revelation in the Bible. See word study: *Dream* at Gen 37:5.

2:2 Chaldeans: Originally a term for Semitic tribes in southern Mesopotamia who helped to build the Neo-Babylonian empire. This appears to be the meaning of the term in 5:30 and 9:1. Here it is used more narrowly, being applied to specialists in astrology and magic who claimed to predict the future by various esoteric arts (2:4, 5, 10). According to the Greek historian Herodotus, Chaldean sages were priests of the god Bel/Marduk (*Histories* 1, 181).

2:4 O king: Beginning with this address, the language of the book switches from Hebrew to Aramaic and continues thus through 7:28. Among various explanations put forward to explain this are the following: (1) It is possible the whole book was written in one language, Hebrew or Aramaic, and only part of it was translated into the other language. Some who adopt this model theorize that while the entire Book of Daniel holds significance for a Jewish readership, and would thus be preserved in Hebrew, chaps. 2–7 are more broadly relevant to Gentile readers, and this could be the reason for keeping or rendering these chapters in Aramaic, which was more widely known. (2) Others, who maintain that Daniel was a book written in stages, suggest that the Aramaic portions are older than the Hebrew portions and were preserved in their original language. (3) Most scholars concede that the rationale for using or preserving two languages has not been satisfactorily explained. **live for ever!:** A royal greeting (3:9; 5:10; 6:6; 1 Kings 1:31; Neh 2:3).

---

[a]Heb adds *in Aramaic*, indicating that the text from this point to the end of chapter 7 is in Aramaic.

"I know with certainty that you are trying to gain time, because you see that the word from me is sure ⁹that if you do not make the dream known to me, there is but one sentence for you. You have agreed to speak lying and corrupt words before me till the times change. Therefore tell me the dream, and I shall know that you can show me its interpretation." ¹⁰The Chalde'ans answered the king, "There is not a man on earth who can meet the king's demand; for no great and powerful king has asked such a thing of any magician or enchanter or Chalde'an. ¹¹The thing that the king asks is difficult, and none can show it to the king except the gods, whose dwelling is not with flesh."

12 Because of this the king was angry and very furious, and commanded that all the wise men of Babylon be destroyed. ¹³So the decree went forth that the wise men were to be slain, and they sought Daniel and his companions, to slay them. ¹⁴Then Daniel replied with prudence and discretion to Ar'ioch, the captain of the king's guard, who had gone out to slay the wise men of Babylon; ¹⁵he said to Ar'ioch, the king's captain, "Why is the decree of the king so severe?" Then Arioch made the matter known to Daniel. ¹⁶And Daniel went in and besought the king to appoint him a time, that he might show to the king the interpretation.

God Reveals Nebuchadnezzar's Dream

17 Then Daniel went to his house and made the matter known to Hanani'ah, Mish'a-el, and Azari'ah, his companions, ¹⁸and told them to seek mercy of the God of heaven concerning this mystery, so that Daniel and his companions might not perish with the rest of the wise men of Babylon. ¹⁹Then the mystery was revealed to Daniel in a vision of the night. Then Daniel blessed the God of heaven. ²⁰Daniel said:

"Blessed be the name of God for ever and ever.
   to whom belong wisdom and might.
²¹He changes times and seasons;
   he removes kings and sets up kings;
  he gives wisdom to the wise
   and knowledge to those who have
    understanding;
²²he reveals deep and mysterious things;
   he knows what is in the darkness,
   and the light dwells with him.
²³To you, O God of my fathers,
   I give thanks and praise,
  for you have given me wisdom and strength,
   and have now made known to me what we
    asked of you,
   for you have made known to us the king's
    matter."

Daniel Interprets the Dream

24 Therefore Daniel went in to Ar'ioch, whom the king had appointed to destroy the wise men of Babylon; he went and said thus to him, "Do not destroy the wise men of Babylon; bring me in before the king, and I will show the king the interpretation."

25 Then Ar'ioch brought in Daniel before the king in haste, and said thus to him: "I have found among the exiles from Judah a man who can make known to the king the interpretation." ²⁶The king said to Daniel, whose name was Belteshaz'zar, "Are you able to make known to me the dream that I have seen and its interpretation?" ²⁷Daniel answered the king, "No wise men, enchanters, magicians, or astrologers can show to the king the mystery which the king has asked, ²⁸but there is a God in heaven who reveals mysteries, and he has made known to King Nebuchadnez'zar what will be in the latter days. Your dream and the visions of your head as you lay in bed are these: ²⁹To you, O king, as you lay

---

2:10 not a man on earth: A confession of the strict limitations of human knowledge. The Babylonian wise men could not have known either the content or the meaning of the king's dreams. Daniel will come to know both, but only as a recipient of divine revelation (2:19, 27–28) (CCC 50–53).

2:18 God of heaven: A popular epithet for God in exilic and postexilic times (Ezra 1:2; Neh 1:4; Tob 10:11; Jud 5:8).

2:28 the latter days: The dream concerns the future. The Aramaic phrase is equivalent to a Hebrew expression that points forward to the age of messianic fulfillment (Num 24:14; Is 2:2; Hos 3:5; cf. Heb 1:2).

Word Study

Mystery (2:18)

Raz (Aram.): a Persian loanword meaning "secret" or "mystery". The term is used in the OT only in the Book of Daniel, where it appears nine times in connection with the dreams of King Nebuchadnezzar of Babylon (Dan 2:18–19, 27–30, 47; 4:9). The mystery refers to the prophetic symbolism encrypted in the king's dreams, which envision the Lord guiding history toward the coming of God's kingdom in the world. Divine revelation is required to understand this (Dan 2:27–28). The association forged between "mystery" and "kingdom" in Daniel seems the most likely backdrop for Jesus' teaching on the mystery of the kingdom of God (Mt 13:11; Mk 4:11). Likewise, Paul probably has this in mind when he relates that the mystery of God's plan for history is fulfilled in Christ's Lordship over the world (Rom 16:25; Eph 1:9; 3:4). Outside the Bible, the Aramaic word *raz* appears in the Dead Sea Scrolls, where it refers to the mysteries of the future (1QS 11, 3), the mysteries of God's ways in heaven (1QM 14, 14), and the mysteries uttered by the biblical Prophets (1QpHab 7, 4).

in bed came thoughts of what would be hereafter, and he who reveals mysteries made known to you what is to be. [30]But as for me, not because of any wisdom that I have more than all the living has this mystery been revealed to me, but in order that the interpretation may be made known to the king, and that you may know the thoughts of your mind.

31 "You saw, O king, and behold, a great image. This image, mighty and of exceeding brightness, stood before you, and its appearance was frightening. [32]The head of this image was of fine gold, its breast and arms of silver, its belly and thighs of bronze, [33]its legs of iron, its feet partly of iron and partly of clay. [34]As you looked, a stone was cut out by no human hand, and it struck the image on its feet of iron and clay, and broke them in pieces; [35]then the iron, the clay, the bronze, the silver, and the gold, all together were broken in pieces, and became like the chaff of the summer threshing floors; and the wind carried them away, so that not a trace of them could be found. But the stone that struck the image became a great mountain and filled the whole earth.

36 "This was the dream; now we will tell the king its interpretation. [37]You, O king, the king of kings, to whom the God of heaven has given the kingdom, the power, and the might, and the glory,

[38]and into whose hand he has given, wherever they dwell, the sons of men, the beasts of the field, and the birds of the air, making you rule over them all—you are the head of gold. [39]After you shall arise another kingdom inferior to you, and yet a third kingdom of bronze, which shall rule over all the earth. [40]And there shall be a fourth kingdom, strong as iron, because iron breaks to pieces and shatters all things; and like iron which crushes, it shall break and crush all these. [41]And as you saw the feet and toes partly of potter's clay and partly of iron, it shall be a divided kingdom; but some of the firmness of iron shall be in it, just as you saw iron mixed with the miry clay. [42]And as the toes of the feet were partly iron and partly clay, so the kingdom shall be partly strong and partly brittle. [43]As you saw the iron mixed with miry clay, so they will mix with one another in marriage,[b] but they will not hold together, just as iron does not mix with clay. [44]And in the days of those kings the God of heaven will set up a kingdom which shall never be destroyed, nor shall its sovereignty be left to another people. It shall break in pieces all these kingdoms and bring them to an end, and it shall stand for ever; [45]just as you saw that a stone was cut from a mountain by no human hand, and that

---

2:44: Rev 11:15.

2:30 not ... wisdom ... I have: Daniel disclaims credit for his knowledge and understanding of the dream. It is not his natural talents or intelligence that makes this possible, but the grace of prophetic illumination. Only God foreknows the course of the future (Is 44:7; Jud 9:5–6) (CCC 2115–17).

2:31–45 Nebuchadnezzar's dream is an allegory of political history in the ancient Near East. The image represents the idolization of earthly power, while its four metals represent four successive empires: Neo-Babylonia (gold), Medo-Persia (silver), Greece (bronze), and Rome (iron). The sequence of metals points to an order of decreasing value as well as increasing strength. In the days of the fourth Gentile empire, the kingdom of God will make its debut (the pulverizing stone) and eventually establish itself everywhere (universal) and for all time (everlasting). Compositionally, the four metals of the dream correspond to the four beasts depicted in 7:1–8. Theologically, the dream reveals Yahweh's control over history, so that even the rise and fall of mighty empires beyond Israel are part of his predetermined plan; likewise, the smashing of the image hints at the downfall of idolatry that will come with the spread of God's kingdom throughout the world. Similar allegories, in which diverse metals represent different ages or kings, appear in Persian (*Bahman Yasht* 1, 2), Greek (Hesiod, *Works and Days* 109–201), and Roman literature (Ovid, *Metamorphoses* 1, 89–150). For an alternative identification of the four metals, see topical essay: *The Four Kingdoms in Daniel*.

2:33 clay: Fired clay or terra cotta, which is brittle (2:42) and unable to bond firmly with iron (2:43). It is a sign of weakness inherent in the fourth empire, which will become "divided" (2:41) despite efforts to unify its dominion (2:43).

2:34 by no human hand: Implies that God himself quarries and hurls the stone. For use of this idiom in the Bible, see topical essay: *Made without Hands* at 2 Cor 5.

2:35 great mountain: Represents the kingdom of God expanding its dominion over the earth. Beyond

this, mountains often held cultic significance in the biblical world, which thought of them as places of contact between heaven and earth. Here one may detect an implied contrast between God's kingdom, not fashioned by human hands, and the artificial mountains of Babylon (called "ziggurats"), which were built as temples for the gods by the hands of countless human laborers (CCC 863). • Israel likewise built its Temple(s) on the mountain height of Jerusalem. The expanding mountain in Daniel recalls the exaltation of Mount Zion, which the prophets expected to grow into the greatest of mountains (Is 2:2–3; Mic 4:1–2). It is from this elevation that Yahweh will reign as King over the world (Is 52:1–10; Mic 4:7). At least one strand of Jewish tradition identified the mountain of Nebuchadnezzar's dream with Zion (*4 Ezra* 13, 36).

2:37 the king of kings: A superlative expression meaning "the greatest king" or "the most powerful king". The NT gives this title to God (1 Tim 6:15) and to Christ (Rev 17:14; 19:16).

2:41 divided kingdom: Signified by the two materials forming the feet of the statue, cast iron and baked clay (2:33).

2:43 mix with one another: An attempt to unify diverse peoples and races that will prove unsuccessful in the long term.

2:44 break in pieces: One Greek translation (Θ) adds "and will crush". In early Christian interpretation, the pulverizing stone is an image of the Messiah who conquers the powers of this world and establishes the universal kingdom of God. • Jesus alludes to this passage when he describes himself as a "stone" that will fall on some and "crush" them (Lk 20:18). • In the final period of these empires, a rock, namely, the Lord and Savior, was cut without hands, which means he was born of a virgin's womb without sexual union or human seed (St. Jerome, *Commentary on Daniel 2*, 40). Other ancient theologians relate the smashing stone to the Second Coming of Christ (St. Hippolytus, *Commentary on Daniel 2*, 13; St. Irenaeus, *Against Heresies* 5, 26, 1–2) (CCC 542, 670, 680).

---

[b] Aramaic *by the seed of men.*

it broke in pieces the iron, the bronze, the clay, the silver, and the gold. A great God has made known to the king what shall be hereafter. The dream is certain, and its interpretation sure."

Daniel and His Friends Promoted

46 Then King Nebuchadnez′zar fell upon his face, and did homage to Daniel, and commanded that an offering and incense be offered up to him. [47]The king said to Daniel, "Truly, your God is God of gods and Lord of kings, and a revealer of mysteries, for you have been able to reveal this mystery." [48]Then the king gave Daniel high honors and many great gifts, and made him ruler over the whole province of Babylon, and chief prefect over all the wise men of Babylon. [49]Daniel made request of the king, and he appointed Shad′rach, Me′shach, and Abed′nego over the affairs of the province of Babylon; but Daniel remained at the king's court.

2:47 your God is God: Full conversion to monotheism is apparently not in view, only an acknowledgment of the greatness and power of the God of Israel. This explains why, in the next chapter, Nebuchadnezzar has no qualms about erecting a national idol.

The Four Kingdoms in Daniel

The Book of Daniel has much to say about Near Eastern politics in the first millennium B.C. The focus of this interest is on a succession of kingdoms that achieved international prominence in the biblical world, beginning with the Neo-Babylonian empire (Dan 2:31–45; 7:1–14). The rise and fall of foreign states might not have interested Daniel's readers except that Israel had been subjugated to each of these Gentile powers in succession.

The question is how to identify which four kingdoms are meant. Virtually all agree that the first is Neo-Babylonia, but disagreement surrounds the three that follow. Many modern scholars identify them as Media, Persia, and Greece. On this reading, the succession of empires came to an end in the second century B.C., when the Maccabean revolt against the Greek kingdom of Syria gave Israel its first taste of political independence in centuries. One can acknowledge certain strengths in this view. For instance, it offers a ready explanation for why some of the visions in Daniel take a particular interest in the Seleucid and Ptolemaic kingdoms founded by the Greek successors of Alexander the Great. Still, this interpretation faces some serious difficulties. Not only did Media never rule as an independent power over the Jewish people, but history is clear that Media was contemporaneous with Neo-Babylonia and not its successor. Media had already been absorbed into the growing Persian kingdom by 550 B.C., more than a decade before Babylon surrendered to Persian forces in 539 B.C. An interpretation that places the Median kingdom *after* Neo-Babylonia seems to require an author beset with a faulty understanding of history or else one who knowingly manipulated the historical facts to fit a theological scheme.

More convincing is the traditional reading, which identifies the four kingdoms as Neo-Babylonia, Medo-Persia, Greece, and Rome. Enumerating empires in this way coheres more closely with the evidence of history as well as the perspective of Daniel's prophecies. Historically, the successor to Neo-Babylonia was Persia, which had already incorporated Media into its expanding base of power. This union is reflected in Daniel by the close association between "the Medes and Persians", who together constitute a single ruling entity (Dan 5:28) that is governed by a single code of law (Dan 6:12, 15) and is represented by a single goat with two horns (Dan 8:20). Likewise, the fourth kingdom is described as "exceedingly strong" (Dan 7:7) and able to "devour the whole earth" (Dan 7:23). This best fits the Roman Empire, which was the greatest imperial force the ancient world had ever seen. Daniel's visions show an awareness of this, indicating that even the armies of the Greek states were defeated and compelled to stand down when faced with the military superiority of the Romans (see notes on Dan 11:18 and 11:30). It is not surprising, then, that Rome was identified as the fourth kingdom of Daniel in a host of ancient Jewish (e.g., Josephus, *Antiquities* 10, 276; *4 Ezra* 11–12; *Leviticus Rabbah* 13, 5; Babylonian Talmud, *Abodah Zarah* 2b) and Christian (e.g., St. Hippolytus, *Commentary on Daniel* 2, 31; St. Cyril of Jerusalem, *Catechesis* 15, 13; St. Jerome, *Commentary on Daniel* 7, 7; Pseudo-Chrysostom, *Interpretation of Daniel* 2, 40) writings.

The Four Empires	Daniel 2	Daniel 7	Daniel 8
Neo-Babylonia (612–539 B.C.)	*Gold Head*	*Lion*	—
Medo-Persia (539–331 B.C.)	*Silver Chest*	*Bear*	*Ram*
Greece (331–63 B.C.)	*Bronze Torso*	*Leopard*	*He-Goat*
Rome (63 B.C.–A.D. 476)	*Iron Legs & Feet*	*Ten-Horned Beast*	—

The Golden Image

3 King Nebuchadnez'zar made an image of gold, whose height was sixty cubits and its breadth six cubits. He set it up on the plain of Dura, in the province of Babylon. ²Then King Nebuchadnez'zar sent to assemble the satraps, the prefects, and the governors, the counselors, the treasurers, the justices, the magistrates, and all the officials of the provinces to come to the dedication of the image which King Nebuchadnezzar had set up. ³Then the satraps, the prefects, and the governors, the counselors, the treasurers, the justices, the magistrates, and all the officials of the provinces, were assembled for the dedication of the image that King Nebuchadnez'zar had set up; and they stood before the image that Nebuchadnezzar had set up. ⁴And the herald proclaimed aloud, "You are commanded, O peoples, nations, and languages, ⁵that when you hear the sound of the horn, pipe, lyre, trigon, harp, bagpipe, and every kind of music, you are to fall down and worship the golden image that King Nebuchadnez'zar has set up; ⁶and whoever does not fall down and worship shall immediately be cast into a burning fiery furnace." ⁷Therefore, as soon as all the peoples heard the sound of the horn, pipe, lyre, trigon, harp, bagpipe, and every kind of music, all the peoples, nations, and languages fell down and worshiped the golden image which King Nebuchadnez'zar had set up.

8 Therefore at that time certain Chalde'ans came forward and maliciously accused the Jews. ⁹They said to King Nebuchadnez'zar, "O king, live for ever! ¹⁰You, O king, have made a decree, that every man who hears the sound of the horn, pipe, lyre, trigon, harp, bagpipe, and every kind of music, shall fall down and worship the golden image; ¹¹and whoever does not fall down and worship shall be cast into a burning fiery furnace. ¹²There are certain Jews whom you have appointed over the affairs of the province of Babylon: Shad'rach, Me'shach, and Abed'nego. These men, O king, pay no heed to you; they do not serve your gods or worship the golden image which you have set up."

13 Then Nebuchadnez'zar in furious rage commanded that Shad'rach, Me'shach, and Abed'nego be brought. Then they brought these men before the king. ¹⁴Nebuchadnez'zar said to them, "Is it true, O Shad'rach, Me'shach, and Abed'nego, that you do not serve my gods or worship the golden image which I have set up? ¹⁵Now if you are ready when you hear the sound of the horn, pipe, lyre, trigon, harp, bagpipe, and every kind of music, to fall down and worship the image which I have made, well and good; but if you do not worship, you shall immediately be cast into a burning fiery furnace; and who is the god that will deliver you out of my hands?"

16 Shad'rach, Me'shach, and Abed'nego answered the king, "O Nebuchadnez'zar, we have no need to answer you in this matter. ¹⁷If it be so, our God whom we serve is able to deliver us from the burning fiery furnace; and he will deliver us out of your hand, O king.ᶜ ¹⁸But if not, be it known to you, O king, that we will not serve your gods or worship the golden image which you have set up."

The Fiery Furnace

19 Then Nebuchadnez'zar was full of fury, and the expression of his face was changed against Shad'rach, Me'shach, and Abed'nego. He ordered the furnace heated seven times more than it was accustomed to be heated. ²⁰And he ordered certain mighty men of his army to bind Shad'rach, Me'shach, and Abed'nego, and to cast them into the burning fiery furnace. ²¹Then these men were bound in their mantles,ᵈ their tunics,ᵈ their hats, and their other garments, and they were cast into

---

3:5, 6: Rev 13:15.

3:1 image of gold: A statue plated with gold (Is 40:19). The colossus, perhaps set on a pedestal, towered 90 feet above the plain. Presumably it represented one of the chief deities of Babylon. **cubits:** One cubit equals about 18 inches, the average length of a man's forearm from elbow to fingertips. **Dura:** The term is nonspecific (it means "enclosure" or "wall") and could refer to one of several sites in Babylonia. Some locate the plain a few miles south of the city of Babylon.

3:4 peoples ... languages: Nebuchadnezzar reigned over a vast multinational empire that encompassed many different cultures and ethnic groups.

3:5 music: Three of the instruments listed have names that are Greek loanwords (lyre, harp, bagpipe). Some consider this evidence that the Book of Daniel appeared in the Hellenistic period, i.e., after 331 B.C., when Alexander the Great diffused Greek language and culture throughout the eastern Mediterranean and beyond. This is possible, but it is not a necessary inference, since elements of Greek culture began to penetrate the Near East as early as the eighth century B.C. **fall down and**

worship: Prostration before the image is mandated as a civic duty toward the State and an expression of loyalty to the king. To the Babylonians, refusal to reverence the idol was as much treasonous as irreligious (3:12).

3:6 fiery furnace: Execution by fire was a known Babylonian practice (Jer 29:22).

3:10 decree: The king's proclamation has the force of law. Its violation is thus deemed a capital crime (3:6, 11).

3:12 certain Jews: Shadrach, Meshach, and Abednego, three friends of Daniel who were promoted to government positions in 2:49. **do not serve ... or worship:** In obedience to the first commandment of the Decalogue, which demands exclusive allegiance to Yahweh and forbids the covenant people to "bow down" before graven images and "serve" them (Ex 20:2–5) (CCC 2112).

3:17 able to deliver us: The young men are confident that Yahweh can rescue them from the wrath of the king. At the same time, they are not presumptuous about the prospect of divine deliverance; they are ready to be martyrs if God wills it (3:18) (CCC 2113).

3:19 seven times more: A hyperbole indicating that the furnace is made "very hot" (3:22). The detail increases the dramatic tension of the story.

ᶜ Or *Behold, our God...king.* Or *If our God is able to deliver us, he will deliver us from the burning fiery furnace and out of your hand, O king.*
ᵈ The meaning of the Aramaic word is uncertain.

the burning fiery furnace. ²²Because the king's order was strict and the furnace very hot, the flame of the fire slew those men who took up Shad′rach, Me′shach, and Abed′nego. ²³And these three men, Shad′rach, Me′shach, and Abed′nego, fell bound into the burning fiery furnace.*

The Prayer of Azariah in the Furnace

1 *And they walked about in the midst of the flames, singing hymns to God and blessing the Lord.* ²*Then Azariah stood and offered this prayer; in the midst of the fire he opened his mouth and said:*

³*"Blessed are you, O Lord, God of our fathers, and worthy of praise;*
and your name is glorified for ever.
⁴*For you are just in all that you have done to us,*
and all your works are true and your ways right,
and all your judgments are truth.
⁵*You have executed true judgments in all that you have brought upon us*
and upon Jerusalem, the holy city of our fathers,
for in truth and justice you have brought all this upon us because of our sins.
⁶*For we have sinfully and lawlessly departed from you,*
and have sinned in all things and have not obeyed your commandments;
⁷*we have not observed them or done them,*
as you have commanded us that it might go well with us.
⁸*So all that you have brought upon us,*
and all that you have done to us,
you have done in true judgment.

⁹*You have given us into the hands of lawless enemies, most hateful rebels,*
and to an unjust king, the most wicked in all the world.
¹⁰*And now we cannot open our mouths;*
shame and disgrace have befallen your servants and worshipers.
¹¹*For your name's sake do not give us up utterly,*
and do not break your covenant,
¹² *and do not withdraw your mercy from us,*
for the sake of Abraham your beloved
and for the sake of Isaac your servant
and Israel your holy one,
¹³*to whom you promised*
to make their descendants as many as the stars of heaven
and as the sand on the shore of the sea.
¹⁴*For we, O Lord, have become fewer than any nation,*
and are brought low this day in all the world because of our sins.
¹⁵*And at this time there is no prince, or prophet, or leader,*
no burnt offering, or sacrifice, or oblation, or incense,
no place to make an offering before you or to find mercy.
¹⁶*Yet with a contrite heart and a humble spirit may we be accepted,*
as though it were with burnt offerings of rams and bulls,
and with tens of thousands of fat lambs;
¹⁷ *such may our sacrifice be in your sight this day,*
and may we wholly follow you,

3:1–68 Two poems stand between verses 23 and 24 of the Aramaic text of Daniel 3: the Prayer of Azariah (*3:1–22* in *italics*) and the Song of the Three Young Men (*3:28–68* in *italics*). These appear in the ancient Greek translations of the OT (LXX and Θ) rather than the Hebrew-Aramaic version of the book (MT), although some evidence suggests they were originally written in a Semitic language. Exactly when these poems first formed part of the Book of Daniel is still undetermined. • The Catholic Church considers the deuterocanonical portions of Daniel to be fully inspired and canonical (Council of Trent, session 4, decree 1). In the Latin Vulgate, the additions are given the verse numbers 3:24–90.

3:2 Azariah: The young Jew renamed "Abednego" in 1:7.

3:3–22 Azariah's prayer is a confession and lament of national sin. It acknowledges Israel's guilt in breaking the

covenant as well as Yahweh's justice in activating the curses of the covenant by dispersing his wayward people into exile (Deut 28:64–68; 29:27–28). So, even though Azariah and his companions have been heroically faithful, the Jewish nation as a whole had been stubbornly unfaithful, and this explains why the three youths are facing persecution and death in a foreign land. Similar confessions appear on the lips of Ezra (Ezra 9:6–15), Nehemiah (Neh 9:6–37), and Daniel (9:4–19).

3:9 lawless enemies The Babylonians. **the most wicked:** From a Jewish perspective, king Nebuchadnezzar earned this infamous reputation when he conquered Jerusalem and burned its Temple to the ground in 586 B.C. (2 Kings 25:8–21).

3:12 for the sake of Abraham: An appeal to God's covenant with Abraham, in which he pledged to multiply the patriarch's descendants (Gen 15:5; 22:16–17).

3:14 fewer than any nation: One of the covenant curses listed in Deut 28:62.

3:15 no prince: The Babylonian conquest of Judah in the sixth century brought about the collapse of the Davidic monarchy. **no place:** With the Temple in ruins, Israel was deprived of its central sanctuary, which alone had been authorized as the place of sacrificial worship (Deut 12:10–14).

3:16 contrite heart: The attitude of one who repents of wrongdoing, recognizes his need for God's mercy, and resolves to mend his ways. Trusting in the words of Psalm 51, Azariah prays that his penitent spirit will be a "sacrifice acceptable to God" (Ps 51:17). For similar statements that compare acts of piety to the cultic offerings of the sanctuary, see Sir 35:1–7 and Acts 10:4 (CCC 1439, 1451–52).

---

*3:23: After this verse the section (sixty-eight verses) printed in italics is contained only in the Greek. It is here translated from Theodotion's version. Concordance of verse numberings:

RSV	Vulgate	RSV	Vulgate
1–28	24–51	*36*	59
29–30	52	*37*	58
31	53	*38–45*	60–67
32	55	*46*	68–69
33	54	*47*	71
34	56	*48*	72
35	57	*49–50*	70
		51–68	73–90

for there will be no shame for those who trust
in you.
[18]And now with all our heart we follow you,
we fear you and seek your face.
[19]Do not put us to shame,
but deal with us in your forbearance
and in your abundant mercy.
[20]Deliver us in accordance with your marvelous
works,
and give glory to your name, O Lord!
Let all who do harm to your servants be put to
shame;
[21]let them be disgraced and deprived of all power
and dominion,
and let their strength be broken.
[22]Let them know that you are the Lord, the only
God,
glorious over the whole world."

[23] Now the king's servants who threw them in did not cease feeding the furnace fires with naphtha, pitch, tow, and brush. [24]And the flame streamed out above the furnace forty-nine cubits, [25]and it broke through and burned those of the Chaldeans whom it caught about the furnace. [26]But the angel of the Lord came down into the furnace to be with Azariah and his companions, and drove the fiery flame out of the furnace, [27]and made the midst of the furnace like a moist whistling wind, so that the fire did not touch them at all or hurt or trouble them.

The Song of the Three Young Men

[28] Then the three, as with one mouth, praised and glorified and blessed God in the furnace, saying:
[29]"Blessed are you, O Lord, God of our fathers,
and to be praised and highly exalted for ever;
[30]And blessed is your glorious, holy name
and to be highly praised and highly exalted for
ever;
[31]Blessed are you in the temple of your holy glory
and to be extolled and highly glorified for ever.
[32]Blessed are you, who sit upon cherubim and look
upon the deeps,
and to be praised and highly exalted for ever.
[33]Blessed are you upon the throne of your kingdom
and to be extolled and highly exalted for ever.
[34]Blessed are you in the firmament of heaven
and to be sung and glorified for ever.

[35]"Bless the Lord, all works of the Lord,
sing praise to him and highly exalt him for
ever.
[36]Bless the Lord, you heavens,
sing praise to him and highly exalt him for
ever.
[37]Bless the Lord, you angels of the Lord,
sing praise to him and highly exalt him for
ever.
[38]Bless the Lord, all waters above the heaven,
sing praise to him and highly exalt him for
ever.
[39]Bless the Lord, all powers,
sing praise to him and highly exalt him for
ever.
[40]Bless the Lord, sun and moon,
sing praise to him and highly exalt him for
ever.
[41]Bless the Lord, stars of heaven,
sing praise to him and highly exalt him for
ever.
[42]Bless the Lord, all rain and dew,
sing praise to him and highly exalt him for
ever.
[43]Bless the Lord, all winds,
sing praise to him and highly exalt him for
ever.
[44]Bless the Lord, fire and heat,
sing praise to him and highly exalt him for
ever.
[45]Bless the Lord, winter cold and summer
heat,
sing praise to him and highly exalt him for
ever.
[46]Bless the Lord, dews and snows,
sing praise to him and highly exalt him for
ever.
[47]Bless the Lord, nights and days,
sing praise to him and highly exalt him for
ever.
[48]Bless the Lord, light and darkness,
sing praise to him and highly exalt him for
ever.
[49]Bless the Lord, ice and cold,
sing praise to him and highly exalt him for
ever.

3:23 naphtha ... brush: Flammable materials used to stoke the furnace and intensify its heat.

3:24 forty-nine cubits: A height of nearly 75 feet. See note on 3:1.

3:28–68 The Song of the Three Young Men. The format and lyrics of the song bring to mind several psalms: its benedictions recall those of Ps 103; its rhythmic use of refrain makes it akin to Ps 136; and its summons for heaven and earth to praise the Lord is reminiscent of Ps 148.

3:30 your ... holy name: Yahweh, the personal name of God. See note on Ex 3:14.

3:31 in the temple: Not the demolished Temple in Jerusalem, but the Lord's celestial Temple in heaven (Ps 11:4; Rev 11:19).

3:32 cherubim: Angels, whose wings form the throne of Yahweh. These were represented in the sanctuaries of Israel by winged figures perched on the lid of the Ark of the Covenant (2 Sam 6:2). See note on Ex 25:18.

3:35 all works of the Lord: Creation is summoned to praise its Creator. The progression of the song moves from heaven and sky (*3:36-41* in *italics*) down through the atmosphere (*3:42-43* in *italics*) to the earth with its weather, seasons, landscape, and inhabitants (*3:44-59* in *italics*). Eventually the focus narrows to man and then to the righteous of Israel in particular (*3:60-66* in *italics*).

3:38 waters above the heaven: Recalls the poetic description of creation in Genesis, where the sky is imagined as a dome that holds up the waters "above the firmament" (Gen 1:7).

⁵⁰*Bless the Lord, frosts and snows,*
  sing praise to him and highly exalt him for
    ever.
⁵¹*Bless the Lord, lightnings and clouds,*
  sing praise to him and highly exalt him for
    ever.
⁵²*Let the earth bless the Lord;*
  let it sing praise to him and highly exalt him
    for ever.
⁵³*Bless the Lord, mountains and hills,*
  sing praise to him and highly exalt him for
    ever.
⁵⁴*Bless the Lord, all things that grow on the earth,*
  sing praise to him and highly exalt him for
    ever.
⁵⁵*Bless the Lord, you springs,*
  sing praise to him and highly exalt him for
    ever.
⁵⁶*Bless the Lord, seas and rivers,*
  sing praise to him and highly exalt him for
    ever.
⁵⁷*Bless the Lord, you whales and all creatures that*
    move in the waters,
  sing praise to him and highly exalt him for
    ever.
⁵⁸*Bless the Lord, all birds of the air,*
  sing praise to him and highly exalt him for
    ever.
⁵⁹*Bless the Lord, all beasts and cattle,*
  sing praise to him and highly exalt him for
    ever.
⁶⁰*Bless the Lord, you sons of men,*
  sing praise to him and highly exalt him for
    ever.
⁶¹*Bless the Lord, O Israel,*
  sing praise to him and highly exalt him for
    ever.
⁶²*Bless the Lord, you priests of the Lord,*
  sing praise to him and highly exalt him for
    ever.
⁶³*Bless the Lord, you servants of the Lord,*
  sing praise to him and highly exalt him for ever.

⁶⁴*Bless the Lord, spirits and souls of the righteous,*
  sing praise to him and highly exalt him for
    ever.
⁶⁵*Bless the Lord, you who are holy and humble in*
    heart,
  sing praise to him and highly exalt him for
    ever.
⁶⁶*Bless the Lord, Hananiah, Azariah, and Mishael,*
  sing praise to him and highly exalt him for
    ever;
  for he has rescued us from Hades and saved us
    from the hand of death,
  and delivered us from the midst of the burning
    fiery furnace;
  from the midst of the fire he has delivered us.
⁶⁷*Give thanks to the Lord, for he is good,*
  for his mercy endures for ever.
⁶⁸*Bless him, all who worship the Lord, the God of*
    gods,
  sing praise to him and give thanks to him,
  for his mercy endures for ever." *

24 Then King Nebuchadnez′zar was astonished and rose up in haste. He said to his counselors, "Did we not cast three men bound into the fire?" They answered the king, "True, O king." ²⁵He answered, "But I see four men loose, walking in the midst of the fire, and they are not hurt; and the appearance of the fourth is like a son of the gods."

The Three Men Are Taken Out of the Furnace

26 Then Nebuchadnez′zar came near to the door of the burning fiery furnace and said, "Shad′rach, Me′shach, and Abed′nego, servants of the Most High God, come forth, and come here!" Then Shadrach, Meshach, and Abednego came out from the fire. ²⁷And the satraps, the prefects, the governors, and the king's counselors gathered together and saw that the fire had not had any power over the bodies of those men; the hair of their heads was not singed, their mantles[d] were not harmed, and no smell of fire had come upon them. ²⁸Nebuchadnez′zar said, "Blessed be the God of Shad′rach, Me′shach, and Abed′nego, who has sent his angel and delivered

---

3:60 sons of men: The human race (Ps 53:2).

3:66 Hananiah, Azariah, and Mishael: The young men address themselves directly in the second person but revert immediately to the first person (we, us, our), as in the beginning of the song (3:29 in *italics*). **Hades:** Greek term for the realm of the dead. For the Hebrew idea behind this, see word study: *Sheol* at Num 16:30.

3:67 Give thanks: A traditional prayer used several times in the OT (1 Chron 16:34; Ps 106:1; 136:1) (CCC 2637–38).

3:25 loose: Only the restraints that "bound" the young men burned off in the flames (3:21). Preserved by faith, their bodies remained unharmed by the fires that raged around them (1 Mac 2:59; Heb 11:34). *a son of the*

gods: i.e., a heavenly being. The fourth figure sighted in the flames is an "angel of the Lord" sent to protect the young men (*3:26* in *italics*; 3:28). Angels are often called "sons of God" in Scripture (Job 1:6; 38:7; Ps 29:1). • The angel or son of God foreshadows the Lord Jesus, who descended into the furnace of Hades, where both sinners and saints were imprisoned, in order that he might deliver those imprisoned by the chains of death without himself suffering any scorching from the fire (St. Jerome, *Commentary on Daniel* 3, 25).

3:26 the Most High: An epithet for Yahweh found often on the lips of Gentiles (Gen 14:19; Num 24:16; Is 14:14).

3:28 yielded up their bodies: One Greek version (Θ) adds "into fire". Daniel's friends choose a fiery death over a cowardly denial of their faith. • Paul may allude to this passage when he claims that surrender of the body to fire is worthless without love, which transforms the laying down of our life into a pleasing sacrifice to God (1 Cor 13:3; cf. Rom 12:1).

---

[d] The meaning of the Aramaic word is uncertain.

*3:68: The reader will notice that the roman figures used for the remaining verses of this chapter take up again the numbering of the protocanonical text. Verses 24–30 are numbered 91–97 in the Greek and Vulgate; they are written in Aramaic, not Hebrew.

his servants, who trusted in him, and set at nothing the king's command, and yielded up their bodies rather than serve and worship any god except their own God. ²⁹Therefore I make a decree: Any people, nation, or language that speaks anything against the God of Shad'rach, Me'shach, and Abed'nego shall be torn limb from limb, and their houses laid in ruins; for there is no other god who is able to deliver in this way." ³⁰Then the king promoted Shad'rach, Me'shach, and Abed'nego in the province of Babylon.

Nebuchadnezzar's Second Dream

4 ^e†King Nebuchadnez'zar to all peoples, nations, and languages, that dwell in all the earth: Peace be multiplied to you! ²It has seemed good to me to show the signs and wonders that the Most High God has wrought toward me.
³How great are his signs,
    how mighty his wonders!
His kingdom is an everlasting kingdom,
    and his dominion is from generation to
        generation.

4 ^f I, Nebuchadnez'zar, was at ease in my house and prospering in my palace. ⁵I had a dream which made me afraid; as I lay in bed the fancies and the visions of my head alarmed me. ⁶Therefore I made a decree that all the wise men of Babylon should be brought before me, that they might make known

to me the interpretation of the dream. ⁷Then the magicians, the enchanters, the Chalde'ans, and the astrologers came in; and I told them the dream, but they could not make known to me its interpretation. ⁸At last Daniel came in before me—he who was named Belteshaz'zar ‡ after the name of my god, and in whom is the spirit of the holy gods^g—and I told him the dream, saying, ⁹"O Belteshaz'zar, chief of the magicians, because I know that the spirit of the holy gods^g is in you and that no mystery is difficult for you, here is^h the dream which I saw; tell me its interpretation. ¹⁰The visions of my head as I lay in bed were these: I saw, and behold, a tree in the midst of the earth; and its height was great. ¹¹The tree grew and became strong, and its top reached to heaven, and it was visible to the end of the whole earth. ¹²Its leaves were fair and its fruit abundant, and in it was food for all. The beasts of the field found shade under it, and the birds of the air dwelt in its branches, and all flesh was fed from it.

13 "I saw in the visions of my head as I lay in bed, and behold, a watcher, a holy one,** came down from heaven. ¹⁴He cried aloud and said thus, 'Hew down the tree and cut off its branches, strip off its leaves and scatter its fruit; let the beasts flee from under it and the birds from its branches. ¹⁵But leave the stump of its roots in the earth, bound with a band of iron and bronze, amid

---

4:12, 21: Ezek 17:23; 31:6; Mt 13:32; Mk 4:32; Lk 13:19.

3:29 decree: An edict of toleration giving legal protection to Judaism in Neo-Babylonia. **no other god:** Nebuchadnezzar marvels at the power of Yahweh to do the impossible (2:46–47). His praise is not a conversion to Jewish monotheism, though it is a public recognition of Yahweh's greatness.

3:30 promoted: Again, fidelity to the Lord in exile brings a reward of blessing and favor in the eyes of the Gentiles (as in 1:8–20 and 2:48–49).

4:1–37 The chapter begins and ends with an autobiographical narrative recited by King Nebuchadnezzar. Notice the use of the first person (I, me, my) in 4:1–18 and then again in 4:34–37. Its opening lines read like the introduction to an epistle or public proclamation (cf. 6:25).

4:1 all peoples: i.e., all those within the Neo-Babylonian empire. See note on 3:4.

4:3 everlasting kingdom: The king learned this when Daniel interpreted his dream about the stone that became an indestructible mountain (2:44).

4:7 Chaldeans: A class of court sages. See note on 2:2. **I told them the dream:** Unlike the earlier episode, where Nebuchadnezzar required the wise men to recount his dream before giving an interpretation (2:2–11).

4:8 Belteshazzar: An abbreviated form of the Babylonian expression "Bel, protect his life". This was the name given to Daniel in 1:7. Bel, meaning "lord", was a title borne by Marduk, the high god of Babylon. **spirit of the holy gods:** Or, "Spirit of the holy God" (see textual note g). One Greek version (Θ) reads: "the holy Spirit of God". • Nebuchadnezzar's words recall Pharaoh's declaration that Joseph, who also interpreted dreams, was indwelt by "the Spirit of God" (Gen 41:38). For other parallels between Daniel and Joseph, see note on 2:1–49.

4:9 mystery: A key concept in Daniel. See word study: *Mystery* at 2:18.

4:10–18 Nebuchadnezzar's dream is a parable of judgment. It warns that his pride will be brought low like a tree that is felled and stripped of its branches and foliage (4:23–25). The banded stump is a sign that his rule can be restored once humility brings him to recognize the sovereignty of God over every earthly dominion (4:26). Archeology has discovered an inscription commissioned by Nebuchadnezzar that describes Babylon as a mighty tree. Here and elsewhere Scripture uses trees to symbolize kingdoms (Ezek 17:22–24; 31:1–18; Mt 13:31–32).

4:11 top reached to heaven: Points to the extreme heights of human pride. This level of arrogance is associated with Babylon and its kings also in Gen 11:4 and Is 14:13–14.

4:13 a watcher: An angel assigned the role of a watchman or sentry (4:17, 23). The term is used of angels only in this chapter of the Bible, though it is often employed in this way in non-biblical Jewish literature (e.g., *1 Enoch, Jubilees, Testaments of the 12 Patriarchs*).

4:15 band of iron: Bands were tightened around the top of a tree stump to prevent the exposed wood from cracking and splitting open. In the symbolism of the dream, this will enable the stump to sprout and grow again (cf. Is 11:1).

---

^eCh 3:31 in Aramaic.
^fCh 4:1 in Aramaic.
^gOr *Spirit of the holy God.*
^hCn: Aramaic *visions of.*
†4:1–3: These verses correspond to 3:31–33 in the Aramaic and to 3:98–100 in the Greek and Vulgate. The chapter is considerably longer in the Greek than in the Aramaic.
‡4:8, *Belteshazzar.* The name given to Daniel means "May Bel protect his life."
**4:13, *a watcher, a holy one*: An angel, so called because he is ever watchful to serve God. In Ezek 1:18 the wheels representing angels are said to be full of eyes.

the tender grass of the field. Let him be wet with the dew of heaven; let his lot be with the beasts in the grass of the earth; [16]let his mind be changed from a man's, and let a beast's mind be given to him; and let seven times pass over him. [17]The sentence is by the decree of the watchers, the decision by the word of the holy ones, to the end that the living may know that the Most High rules the kingdom of men, and gives it to whom he will, and sets over it the lowliest of men.' [18]This dream I, King Nebuchadnez'zar, saw. And you, O Belteshaz'zar, declare the interpretation, because all the wise men of my kingdom are not able to make known to me the interpretation, but you are able, for the spirit of the holy gods[1] is in you."

Daniel Interprets the Second Dream

19 Then Daniel, whose name was Belteshaz'zar, was dismayed for a moment, and his thoughts alarmed him. The king said, "Belteshaz'zar, let not the dream or the interpretation alarm you." Belteshazzar answered, "My lord, may the dream be for those who hate you and its interpretation for your enemies! [20]The tree you saw, which grew and became strong, so that its top reached to heaven, and it was visible to the end of the whole earth; [21]whose leaves were fair and its fruit abundant, and in which was food for all; under which beasts of the field found shade, and in whose branches the birds of the air dwelt— [22]it is you, O king, who have grown and become strong. Your greatness has grown and reaches to heaven, and your dominion to the ends of the earth. [23]And whereas the king saw a watcher, a holy one, coming down from heaven and saying, 'Hew down the tree and destroy it, but leave the stump of its roots in the earth, bound with a band of iron and bronze, in the tender grass of the field; and let him be wet with the dew of heaven; and let his lot be with the beasts of the field, till seven times pass over him'; [24]this is the interpretation, O king: It is a decree of the Most High, which has come upon

my lord the king, [25]that you shall be driven from among men, and your dwelling shall be with the beasts of the field; you shall be made to eat grass like an ox, and you shall be wet with the dew of heaven, and seven times shall pass over you, till you know that the Most High rules the kingdom of men, and gives it to whom he will. [26]And as it was commanded to leave the stump of the roots of the tree, your kingdom shall be sure for you from the time that you know that Heaven rules. [27]Therefore, O king, let my counsel be acceptable to you; break off your sins by practicing righteousness, and your iniquities by showing mercy to the oppressed, that there may perhaps be a lengthening of your tranquillity."

28 All this came upon King Nebuchadnez'zar. [29]At the end of twelve months he was walking on the roof of the royal palace of Babylon, [30]and the king said, "Is not this great Babylon, which I have built by my mighty power as a royal residence and for the glory of my majesty?" [31]While the words were still in the king's mouth, there fell a voice from heaven, "O King Nebuchadnez'zar, to you it is spoken: The kingdom has departed from you, [32]and you shall be driven from among men, and your dwelling shall be with the beasts of the field; and you shall be made to eat grass like an ox; and seven times shall pass over you, until you have learned that the Most High rules the kingdom of men and gives it to whom he will." [33]Immediately the word was fulfilled upon Nebuchadnez'zar. He was driven from among men, and ate grass like an ox, and his body was wet with the dew of heaven till his hair grew as long as eagles' feathers, and his nails were like birds' claws.

Nebuchadnezzar Praises God

34 At the end of the days I, Nebuchadnez'zar, lifted my eyes to heaven, and my reason returned to me, and I blessed the Most High, and praised and honored him who lives for ever;

4:16 times: Possibly years, but this is uncertain because the text does not specify the duration of the king's insanity in conventional terms.

4:25 like an ox: Modern psychiatry defines this as *boanthropy*, a rare mental illness in which the victim thinks himself a bovine and acts accordingly. Babylonian sources say nothing of these seven years (or months) of insanity, but little is known about Nebuchadnezzar's reign and activities from 593 to 562 B.C. This could be a simple accident of history; on the other hand, court historians, for political and other reasons, might well have reason to suppress information about a king's mental incapacities. Interestingly, Josephus, the Jewish historian, quotes the work of a Babylonian priest who indicated that Nebuchadnezzar suffered from an illness late in his reign (*Against Apion* 1, 146).

4:26 Heaven: A Jewish expression for "God" (13:9; 1 Mac 3:18–19; 4:10).

✠ **4:27 break off your sins:** Or, "redeem your sins". Daniel's advice expresses the early Jewish belief that sin creates a debt in heaven and that works of righteousness

generate a treasury of credit or merit with God (Tob 4:7–11; Sir 29:9–13). The sinful Nebuchadnezzar has racked up a significant spiritual debt that can be paid down by giving to the poor, which counts as giving or lending to the Lord (Prov 19:17). The benefits of almsgiving and similar acts of charity include remission of sin (Tob 12:9; Sir 3:30) and rescue from times of trouble (Tob 14:11; Sir 40:24). Belief in a treasury in heaven, funded by generosity toward the needy, carried over into the teaching of Jesus (Mt 6:19–20; 19:21) and the early Church (*Didache* 4, 5–7) (CCC 1434, 2447, 2462). • God is satisfied by works of justice, and sins are washed away by the merits of mercy. Daniel prescribed such a remedy for avoiding evils. But when King Nebuchadnezzar refused to comply, he was beset with misfortunes that he could have averted had he redeemed his sins by almsgiving (St. Cyprian, *On Works and Alms* 5).

4:32 until you have learned: The aim of divine judgment is remedial, i.e., it is meant to teach humility and induce repentance. In the case of Nebuchadnezzar, it has its intended effect (4:34–37).

4:34 everlasting dominion: Reiterates the praises of God in 4:2–3.

---

[1] Or *Spirit of the holy God.*

for his dominion is an everlasting dominion,
> and his kingdom endures from generation to
> generation;

[35]all the inhabitants of the earth are accounted as
> nothing;
> and he does according to his will in the host of
> heaven
> and among the inhabitants of the earth;
> and none can stay his hand
> or say to him, "What have you done?"

[36]At the same time my reason returned to me; and for the glory of my kingdom, my majesty and splendor returned to me. My counselors and my lords sought me, and I was established in my kingdom, and still more greatness was added to me. [37]Now I, Nebuchadnez′zar, praise and extol and honor the King of heaven; for all his works are right and his ways are just; and those who walk in pride he is able to abase.

Belshazzar's Feast

5 King Belshaz′zar* made a great feast for a thousand of his lords, and drank wine in front of the thousand.

2 Belshaz′zar, when he tasted the wine, commanded that the vessels of gold and of silver which Nebuchadnez′zar his father had taken out of the temple in Jerusalem be brought, that the king and his lords, his wives, and his concubines might drink from them. [3]Then they brought in the golden and silver vessels[j] which had been taken out of the temple, the house of God in Jerusalem; and the king and his lords, his wives, and his concubines drank from them. [4]They drank wine, and praised the gods of gold and silver, bronze, iron, wood, and stone.

The Handwriting on the Wall

5 Immediately the fingers of a man's hand appeared and wrote on the plaster of the wall of the king's palace, opposite the lampstand; and the king saw the hand as it wrote. [6]Then the king's color changed, and his thoughts alarmed him; his limbs gave way, and his knees knocked together. [7]The king cried aloud to bring in the enchanters, the Chalde′ans, and the astrologers. The king said to the wise men of Babylon, "Whoever reads this writing, and shows me its interpretation, shall be clothed with purple, and have a chain of gold about his neck, and shall be the third ruler in the kingdom." [8]Then all the king's wise men came in, but they could not read the writing or make known to the king the interpretation. [9]Then King Belshaz′zar was greatly alarmed, and his color changed; and his lords were perplexed.

10 The queen, because of the words of the king and his lords, came into the banqueting hall; and the queen said, "O king, live for ever! Let not your thoughts alarm you or your color change. [11]There is in your kingdom a man in whom is the spirit of the holy gods.[k] In the days of your father light and understanding and wisdom, like the wisdom of the gods, were found in him, and King Nebuchadnez′zar, your father, made him chief of the magicians, enchanters, Chalde′ans, and astrologers,[l] [12]because an excellent spirit, knowledge, and understanding to interpret dreams, explain riddles, and solve problems were found in this Daniel, whom the king named Belteshaz′zar. Now let Daniel be called, and he will show the interpretation."

4:37 walk in pride ... abase: The moral of the story is summarized here in its last line.

5:1–29 Daniel again upstages the wise men of Babylon in a contest of wisdom. This time the king summons him to interpret, not a dream, as in chaps. 2 and 4, but mysterious handwriting scrawled on the palace wall. More than two decades separate the events in chaps. 4 and 5.

5:1 Belshazzar: The name means "Bel, protect the king". Strictly speaking, Belshazzar was a crown prince and deputy regent rather than the king of Neo-Babylonia—a title officially borne by his father, Nabonidus, who reigned from 556 to 539 B.C. However, because Nabonidus withdrew from Babylon to reside in western Arabia (Teima) for the latter half of his reign, Belshazzar did in fact exercise royal authority during his father's absence. This situation is presupposed in Daniel, for Belshazzar can only offer to make the interpreter of the writing "third ruler" in the kingdom (5:7, 16, 29). In other words, the highest position available at that time was under the king (Nabonidus) and his deputy regent (Belshazzar). **great feast:** Greek historians tell us that Babylonian banquets were often times of sexual and idolatrous revelry.

5:2 the vessels: Liturgical cups, bowls, and flasks that were confiscated from the Temple in Jerusalem. See note on 1:2. **his father:** A degree of uncertainty surrounds this reputed relationship (also noted in Bar 1:1). Historians often contend that Nebuchadnezzar was not a biological ancestor of Belshazzar, although some have interpreted the evidence to indicate that Belshazzar's mother was Nebuchadnezzar's daughter. Another possibility, suggested by the Semitic custom of giving kinship terms an application broader than blood ties, is that "father" in this case means "predecessor".

5:4 praised the gods: Insult is added to injury when the Temple vessels, already defiled by profane use, are employed in the worship of Babylon's idols. **gold ... silver ... bronze ... iron:** Recalls the metals of the image in Nebuchadnezzar's dream (2:31–33).

5:5 Immediately: The Lord is quick to respond to this sacrilegious mockery.

5:7 purple: A color associated with royalty (Esther 8:15; Mk 15:17). **chain of gold:** An emblem of ruling authority (Gen 41:42). **third ruler:** The highest government position open at the time. See note on 5:1.

5:10 the queen: Not one of the wives of Belshazzar, for his female consorts were already present in the banquet hall (5:3). The conventions of queenship in the ancient Near East suggest that she was his mother or grandmother. See essay: *Queen Mother* at 1 Kings 2.

5:11 spirit of the holy gods: On this expression, see note on 4:8.

---

[j] Theodotion Vg: Aramaic *golden vessels.*
[k] Or *Spirit of the holy God.*
[l] Aramaic repeats *the king your father.*
*5:1, *Belshazzar*: He was the son of Nabonidus and was never in fact king.

Daniel Interprets the Writing on the Wall

13 Then Daniel was brought in before the king. The king said to Daniel, "You are that Daniel, one of the exiles of Judah, whom the king my father brought from Judah. [14]I have heard of you that the spirit of the holy gods[k] is in you, and that light and understanding and excellent wisdom are found in you. [15]Now the wise men, the enchanters, have been brought in before me to read this writing and make known to me its interpretation; but they could not show the interpretation of the matter. [16]But I have heard that you can give interpretations and solve problems. Now if you can read the writing and make known to me its interpretation, you shall be clothed with purple, and have a chain of gold about your neck, and shall be the third ruler in the kingdom."

17 Then Daniel answered before the king, "Let your gifts be for yourself, and give your rewards to another; nevertheless I will read the writing to the king and make known to him the interpretation. [18]O king, the Most High God gave Nebuchadnez′zar your father kingship and greatness and glory and majesty; [19]and because of the greatness that he gave him, all peoples, nations, and languages trembled and feared before him; whom he would he slew, and whom he would he kept alive; whom he would he raised up, and whom he would he put down. [20]But when his heart was lifted up and his spirit was hardened so that he dealt proudly, he was deposed from his kingly throne, and his glory was taken from him; [21]he was driven from among men, and his mind was made like that of a beast, and his dwelling was with the wild donkeys; he was fed grass like an ox, and his body was wet with the dew of heaven, until he knew that the Most High God rules the kingdom of men, and sets over it whom he will. [22]And you his son, Belshaz′zar, have not humbled your heart, though you knew all this, [23]but you have lifted up yourself against the Lord of heaven; and the vessels of his house have been brought in before you, and you and your lords, your wives, and your concubines have drunk wine from them; and you have praised the gods of silver and gold, of bronze, iron, wood, and stone, which do not see or hear or know, but the God in whose hand is your breath, and whose are all your ways, you have not honored.

24 "Then from his presence the hand was sent, and this writing was inscribed. [25]And this is the writing that was inscribed: MENE, MENE, TEKEL, and PARSIN. [26]This is the interpretation of the matter: MENE, God has numbered the days of your kingdom and brought it to an end; [27]TEKEL, you have been weighed in the balances and found wanting; [28]PERES, your kingdom is divided and given to the Medes and Persians."

29 Then Belshaz′zar commanded, and Daniel was clothed with purple, a chain of gold was put about his neck, and proclamation was made concerning him, that he should be the third ruler in the kingdom.

30 That very night Belshaz′zar the Chalde′an king was slain. [31]And Dari′us the Mede* received the kingdom, being about sixty-two years old.

5:13 one of the exiles: Daniel was taken captive to Babylon in 605 B.C. (1:1–6).

5:18 God gave ... kingship: Yahweh exercises absolute sovereignty over world powers.

5:20–21 Nebuchadnezzar's insolence and insanity are recounted in chap. 4.

5:22–23 Belshazzar is declared guilty of arrogance (exalting himself above the Lord), profanation (defiling the Temple vessels), sacrilege (praising idols with liturgical vessels consecrated to Yahweh), and failing to learn the spiritual lessons of history (God had punished the pride of Nebuchadnezzar with temporary insanity).

5:23 do not see or hear: Several taunts against idols in the Bible stress the point that man-made images are not living beings with intelligence or sensory perceptions (Ps 115:4–7; Jer 10:1–10; Hab 2:18–19) (CCC 2112).

5:25 MENE, TEKEL, and PARSIN: The cryptic message relates to three monetary weights or units: the *mina*, the *shekel*, and the *parsa*. In this context, the language of commercial transaction points to the political transition soon to result from Persia's conquest of Babylon. Daniel reinforces this message of judgment with a series of verbal puns: MENE resembles a verb meaning "to number"; TEKEL resembles a verb meaning "to weigh"; and PARSIN resembles a verb meaning "to divide" as well as the noun for "Persians".

5:28 Medes and Persians: Peoples of ancient Iran who lived north and east of Babylonia. Both were migrant peoples, and both began life in the region as independent states, but by 550 B.C. the Persians, under the leadership of Cyrus II the Great, had seized control of Media and absorbed it into its expanding empire. By 539 B.C., the Medo-Persian kingdom became the successor to Neo-Babylonia as the imperial superpower of the Near East. See essay: *The Four Kingdoms in Daniel* at Dan 2.

5:30 Chaldean: The ethnic identity of the king. See note on 2:2. **slain:** Xenophon likewise reports that Persian troops killed the king of Babylon when the city was taken in 539 B.C. (*Cyropaedia* 7, 5, 32–33).

5:31 Darius the Mede: No figure of this name is known to history outside the Book of Daniel, which identifies him as a "Mede" who became "king" over the Neo-Babylonian realm after the fall of Babylon in 539 B.C. (9:1). Modern scholarship has often declared Darius the Mede a fictional character (representing the kingdom of Media as distinct from Persia) or has treated the matter as a case of mistaken identity (the author having confused him with Darius I Hystaspes, ruler of Persia from 522 to 486 B.C.). Scholars who accept the historicity of Daniel have identified Darius the Mede with a person known to history under another name. Three major attempts at identification have been made. (1) Some have identified Darius with *Gubaru*, the man Cyrus II of Persia made governor of Babylon and satrap of the Persian province west of the Euphrates. He was not a king in any strict sense, but he wielded considerable power under Cyrus, and some have read the passive expression in 9:1 as confirming that he was appointed by a higher authority. (2) Others have identified Darius with the elderly general *Ugbaru*, who orchestrated the Persian conquest of Babylon. He lived only a short time after victory over Babylon was achieved but long enough to have been promoted to high

---

[k]Or *Spirit of the holy God.*

*5:31, *Darius the Mede*: Nothing is known in history of this person. The Persians, moreover, had already conquered the Medes before taking Babylon.

A Plot against Daniel

6 It pleased Dari'us to set over the kingdom a hundred and twenty satraps, to be throughout the whole kingdom; [2]and over them three presidents, of whom Daniel was one, to whom these satraps should give account, so that the king might suffer no loss. [3]Then this Daniel became distinguished above all the other presidents and satraps, because an excellent spirit was in him; and the king planned to set him over the whole kingdom. [4]Then the presidents and the satraps sought to find a ground for complaint against Daniel with regard to the kingdom; but they could find no ground for complaint or any fault, because he was faithful, and no error or fault was found in him. [5]Then these men said, "We shall not find any ground for complaint against this Daniel unless we find it in connection with the law of his God."

6 Then these presidents and satraps came by agreement[m] to the king and said to him, "O King Dari'us, live for ever! [7]All the presidents of the kingdom, the prefects and the satraps, the counselors and the governors are agreed that the king should establish an ordinance and enforce an interdict, that whoever makes petition to any god or man for thirty days, except to you, O king, shall be cast into the den of lions. [8]Now, O king, establish the interdict and sign the document, so that it cannot be changed, according to the law of the Medes and the Persians, which cannot be revoked." [9]Therefore King Dari'us signed the document and interdict.

Daniel in the Den of Lions

10 When Daniel knew that the document had been signed, he went to his house where he had windows in his upper chamber open toward Jerusalem; and he got down upon his knees three times a day and prayed and gave thanks before his God, as he had done previously. [11]Then these men came by agreement[m] and found Daniel making petition and supplication before his God. [12]Then they came near and said before the king, concerning the interdict, "O king! Did you not sign an interdict, that any man who makes petition to any god or man within thirty days except to you, O king, shall be cast into the den of lions?" The king answered, "The thing stands fast, according to the law of the Medes and Persians, which cannot be revoked." [13]Then they answered before the king, "That Daniel, who is one of the exiles from Judah, pays no heed to you, O king, or the interdict you have signed, but makes his petition three times a day."

14 Then the king, when he heard these words, was much distressed, and set his mind to deliver Daniel; and he labored till the sun went down to rescue him. [15]Then these men came by agreement[m] to the king, and said to the king, "Know, O king, that it is a law of the Medes and Persians that no interdict or ordinance which the king establishes can be changed."

16 Then the king commanded, and Daniel was brought and cast into the den of lions. The king said to Daniel, "May your God, whom you serve

---

government office. (3) Still others have identified Darius as *Cyrus II* himself, whom extrabiblical sources list as the conqueror of Babylon, as a king advanced in years, and as one descended from the royal houses of Media (mother's side) and Persia (father's side). Advocates point out that the Hebrew conjunction "and" in 6:28 can also be read as an explicative (translating "namely" or "that is"), thus identifying Darius and Cyrus as one and the same person. Some who argue for this identification suggest that "Darius" was simply a throne name borne by Cyrus in Babylon.

6:1-28 Daniel's rescue from the lions' den is the last of the court tales that make up the first part of the book. Chap. 6 mirrors the conflict and resolution of chap. 3: in both, Jewish exiles hold official positions in a Near Eastern government (3:12; 6:1-3); a royal decree is issued that contradicts their faith (3:4-6; 6:6-9); the heroes remain faithful to the Lord despite the prospect of death (3:16-18; 6:10); they are punished as criminals but are saved by an angel (3:24-28; 6:22); and the king publically admires the saving power of Yahweh (3:29; 6:25-27).

6:1 satraps: Governors of major Persian provinces. The reference to 120 satraps probably includes, not only the administrators of the major provinces or satrapies, but rulers of the subdistricts within each (cf. Esther 1:1).

6:2 three presidents: A triumvirate of senior officials overseeing the satrapies.

6:3 over the whole kingdom: Daniel is on track for promotion as the prime minister of the Medo-Persian empire. For the prominence of this position in the biblical world, see word study: *Over the Household* at 1 Kings 16:9.

6:4 sought to find: A political conspiracy develops to oust Daniel from his current position despite his impeccable service record.

6:7 den of lions: A large pit with steep sides and a small opening at ground level. Hungry lions prowled in the darkness below (6:24), and a heavy stone was used to block the overhead entrance (6:17). Unlike the Babylonians, who executed criminals by fire (3:6; Jer 29:22), the Persians used other means, since fire was a sacred medium for drawing near to their creator god, Ahura-Mazda. The shift in methods of capital punishment from chap. 3 (Babylonian) to chap. 6 (Persian) may thus be taken as a sign of historical authenticity.

6:8 cannot be changed: Decrees signed into law by the king were irrevocable in the Medo-Persian empire (6:12, 15; Esther 1:19; 8:8).

6:10 his house: Not normally open to the prying eyes of others. • We learn from this passage not to expose ourselves unnecessarily to danger; rather, so far as it lies with us, we should avoid the schemes of our enemies. In Daniel's case, he goes against the king's authority, not in a public setting, but rather in a private place, so as not to neglect the commands of the one true God (St. Jerome, *Commentary on Daniel* 6, 11). **toward Jerusalem:** Prayer in the direction of the Holy City was inspired by Solomon's words at the dedication of the Temple (1 Kings 8:29; Ps 5:7; 138:2). **upon his knees:** Scripture widely attests the practice of kneeling for prayer (1 Kings 8:54; Ezra 9:5; Ps 95:6; Lk 22:41; Acts 20:36). **three times a day:** Probably morning, midday, and evening (Ps 55:17).

---

[m] Or *thronging*.

continually, deliver you!" [17]And a stone was brought and laid upon the mouth of the den, and the king sealed it with his own signet and with the signet of his lords, that nothing might be changed concerning Daniel. [18]Then the king went to his palace, and spent the night fasting; no diversions were brought to him, and sleep fled from him.

God Saves Daniel from the Lions

19 Then, at break of day, the king arose and went in haste to the den of lions. [20]When he came near to the den where Daniel was, he cried out in a tone of anguish and said to Daniel, "O Daniel, servant of the living God, has your God, whom you serve continually, been able to deliver you from the lions?" [21]Then Daniel said to the king, "O king, live for ever! [22]My God sent his angel and shut the lions' mouths, and they have not hurt me, because I was found blameless before him; and also before you, O king, I have done no wrong." [23]Then the king was exceedingly glad, and commanded that Daniel be taken up out of the den. So Daniel was taken up out of the den, and no kind of hurt was found upon him, because he had trusted in his God. [24]And the king commanded, and those men who had accused Daniel were brought and cast into the den of lions— they, their children, and their wives; and before they reached the bottom of the den the lions overpowered them and broke all their bones in pieces.

25 Then King Dari'us wrote to all the peoples, nations, and languages that dwell in all the earth: "Peace be multiplied to you. [26]I make a decree, that in all my royal dominion men tremble and fear before the God of Daniel,

for he is the living God,
enduring for ever;
his kingdom shall never be destroyed,
and his dominion shall be to the end.
[27]He delivers and rescues,
he works signs and wonders
in heaven and on earth,
he who has saved Daniel
from the power of the lions."

28 So this Daniel prospered during the reign of Dari'us and the reign of Cyrus the Persian.

Visions of the Four Beasts
and the Ancient of Days

7 In the first year of Belshaz'zar king of Babylon, Daniel had a dream and visions of his head as he lay in his bed. Then he wrote down the dream, and told the sum of the matter. [2]Daniel said, "I saw in my vision by night, and behold, the four winds of heaven were stirring up the great sea. [3]And four great beasts came up out of the sea, different from one another. [4]The first was like a lion and had eagles' wings. Then as I looked its wings were plucked off, and it was lifted up from the ground and made to stand upon two feet like a man; and the mind of a man was given to it. [5]And behold, another beast, a second one, like a bear. It was raised up on one side; it had three ribs in its mouth between its teeth; and it was told, 'Arise, devour much flesh.' [6]After this I looked, and behold,

---

6:22: 2 Tim 4:17.   **7:3:** Rev 13:1.   **7:3, 7, 21:** Rev 11:7.   **7:4-6:** Rev 13:2.

6:17 sealed it: The king pressed his signet, engraved with royal insignia, into a wax or clay bond. So long as the seal impression was intact, it could be verified that no one had tampered with the cover stone and thus acted against the king's authority. A similar procedure was used to seal the stone that blocked the entrance to Jesus' tomb (Mt 27:66).

6:22 shut the lions' mouths: A divine miracle accomplished through an angel. It is a testimony, not only to God's power over the animal kingdom, but to the innocence of Daniel (1 Mac 2:60), whose extraordinary faith "stopped the mouths of lions" (Heb 11:33). **before him ... before you:** Daniel is a saint as well as a model citizen.

6:24 children ... wives: It seems to have been Persian custom to punish the entire family of a convicted criminal (cf. Esther 9:13-14).

6:25-27 The proclamation of Darius the Mede, delivered in the form of a royal epistle, parallels the proclamation of Nebuchadnezzar in 4:1-3.

6:28 and: The Hebrew conjunction is here translated as a connective ("and"), although it could also be read as an explicative ("namely" or "that is"). For the possible significance of this, see note on 5:31.

7:1-28 The first of Daniel's four visions. It adapts the traditional Semitic motif of a warrior god who conquers the chaos of the sea and then claims the reward of kingship (known as the "combat myth"). Theologically, the vision is fully conformed to Israel's faith in Yahweh as the Victor over evil and chaos in the world (cf. Job 26:12-13; Ps 74:12-14; Is 27:1).

7:1 first year: Exact date uncertain but ca. 552 B.C. This is approximately when Belshazzar became deputy regent of Babylon in his father's absence. See note on 5:1.

7:2-8 Daniel's dream, which features four beasts from the sea, parallels Nebuchadnezzar's dream, which surveys the four metals of a statue (2:31-35). Both represent a succession of Near Eastern empires that gives way to the messianic kingdom of God. Jewish and Christian tradition typically identify (1) the winged lion as *Neo-Babylonia*, often depicted as a sphinx in Mesopotamian art; (2) the bear as *Medo-Persia*, the three ribs in its teeth being its three major conquests of Lydia (547 B.C.), Babylon (539 B.C.), and Egypt (525 B.C.); (3) the leopard as *Greece*, which enlarged its dominion with incredible speed, having four wings and heads representing the four generals of Alexander the Great who inherited his vast empire; and (4) the indescribable beast as *Rome*, whose horns are its emperors and whose territory and military might surpassed all predecessors. Alternatively, many modern scholars identify the four kingdoms as Neo-Babylonia, Media, Persia, and Greece. From a Jewish perspective, the zoological images are those of unclean animals (Lev 11:13, 27). See topical essay: *The Four Kingdoms in Daniel* at Dan 2.

7:2 the great sea: The Mediterranean Sea (Num 34:6; Ezek 47:10). Jewish readers would thus envision the beasts making landfall on the western coast of Israel.

7:4 the mind of a man: An allusion to Nebuchadnezzar's recovery from madness (4:34) after a time of living like a beast (4:33).

7:5 raised up on one side: Probably symbolizes Persia's dominance in the Medo-Persian empire. The same point is made in Daniel's next vision, where Medo-Persia appears as a ram with one horn "higher than the other" (8:3).

another, like a leopard, with four wings of a bird on its back; and the beast had four heads; and dominion was given to it. [7]After this I saw in the night visions, and behold, a fourth beast, terrifying and dreadful and exceedingly strong; and it had great iron teeth; it devoured and broke in pieces, and stamped the residue with its feet. It was different from all the beasts that were before it; and it had ten horns. [8]I considered the horns, and behold, there came up among them another horn, a little one,* before which three of the first horns were plucked up by the roots; and behold, in this horn were eyes like the eyes of a man, and a mouth speaking great things. [9]As I looked,

> thrones were placed
>> and one that was ancient of days took his seat;
> his clothing was white as snow,
>> and the hair of his head like pure wool;
> his throne was fiery flames,
>> its wheels were burning fire.
> [10]A stream of fire issued
>> and came forth from before him;
> a thousand thousands served him,

> and ten thousand times ten thousand stood
>> before him;
> the court sat in judgment,
>> and the books were opened.

[11]I looked then because of the sound of the great words which the horn was speaking. And as I looked, the beast was slain, and its body destroyed and given over to be burned with fire. [12]As for the rest of the beasts, their dominion was taken away, but their lives were prolonged for a season and a time. [13]I saw in the night visions,

> and behold, with the clouds of heaven
>> there came one like a son of man, †
> and he came to the Ancient of Days
>> and was presented before him.
> [14]And to him was given dominion
>> and glory and kingdom,
> that all peoples, nations, and languages
>> should serve him;
> his dominion is an everlasting dominion,
>> which shall not pass away,
> and his kingdom one
>> that shall not be destroyed.

7:7: Rev 12:3; 13:1; 17:3. **7:8, 11:** Rev 13:5. **7:9:** Rev 1:14; 20:4, 11. **7:10:** Rev 5:11; 20:12. **7:13–14:** Mt 24:30; 26:64; Mk 13:26; 14:62; Lk 21:27; 22:69; Rev 1:7, 13; 14:14. **7:14, 18, 22, 27:** Rev 11:15.

7:7 iron teeth: Recalls the iron legs and feet of the statue seen by Nebuchadnezzar (2:33).

7:8 a little one: A king who speaks boastful words (7:11) and wages war against the saints of God (7:21). Supposing the fourth beast represents Rome, the best candidate is Caesar Nero (A.D. 54 to 68), the first Roman emperor to instigate a savage persecution of the Church (Tacitus, *Annals* 15, 44). The Book of Revelation depicts Nero, whose name has the numerical value 666, as the beast that rises from the sea (Rev 13:1) and utters "haughty and blasphemous words" against the Lord (Rev 13:5). Those who identify the fourth beast with Greece relate the little horn to Antiochus IV Epiphanes (175 to 164 B.C.), who appears under this image in a later vision (8:9) and who too speaks "astonishing things" against God (11:36). • Christian tradition has seen in the little horn of Daniel 7 the dreadful features of the future Antichrist (e.g., St. Augustine, *City of God* 20, 23) (CCC 675–76). See note on 7:2–8.

7:9–10 The courtroom of heaven. The presiding Judge is the Ancient of Days (= Yahweh); his attendants are the thousand thousands (= host of angels); and the books opened for examination are volumes that record the deeds of men (Ps 56:8; Mal 3:16; Rev 20:12) (CCC 678).

7:9 throne ... its wheels: The Lord is seated on a chariot throne (Ezek 1:15–28), which was represented in Israel's Temple by the Ark of the Covenant (1 Chron 28:18).

7:11 burned with fire: Flames of judgment stream from the divine throne (7:10; Ps 97:3). • In the Book of Revelation, the beast from the sea (Rome) is eventually hurled into a lake of fire (Rev 19:20; cf. *4 Ezra* 12, 3).

7:13 clouds of heaven: Often associated with divinity in the biblical world. God manifests his glory in the form of a dense cloud (Ex 16:10; 24:15–18; 40:34; 1

Kings 8:10–11; Is 4:5) and is sometimes pictured riding the clouds as his war chariot (Ps 68:4; 104:3; Is 19:1). The latter image recalls a popular motif in Canaanite mythology, where the storm god Baal bore the title "Rider of the Clouds". **son of man:** Normally this expression refers to a mortal human being (8:17; Ps 8:4; 146:3). Here the term is part of a simile: the figure is *like* a man in appearance, yet his identity is not reducible to a mere mortal. He is an exalted figure who comes on the clouds of heavenly glory to receive an everlasting kingship. Some identify the Danielic "son of man" as an angel (e.g., Michael) or as a symbol of the People of God (the faithful of Israel). More likely, he is a messianic figure and mediator who comes before God as a representative of the saints on earth, with whom he shares his dominion (7:18, 22, 27). Ancient Jewish tradition identified the "son of man" in Daniel's vision with a heavenly Messiah and Son of God (*1 Enoch* 46, 1–3; 48, 2–10; 52, 10; *4 Ezra* 13, 1–32; *Numbers Rabbah* 7, 13; Babylonian Talmud, *Sanhedrin* 96b–97a). • In the Gospels, Jesus adopts a messianic interpretation when he identifies himself as the "Son of man" whose enthronement in heaven coincides with a time of judgment on earth (Mk 14:61–62; cf. Mt 16:27–28; 24:30–31; Acts 7:55–56; Rev 14:14). Jesus likewise reenacts the scenario in Daniel when he entrusts his kingdom to his apostles and disciples, i.e., to the saints of the New Covenant (Lk 12:32; 22:28–30) (CCC 440, 664). See topical essay: *Jesus, the Son of Man* at Lk 17. • The words "like a son of man" show that Christ would become man and appear in this way, yet he would not be born of human seed. Daniel pronounced the same truth in a figurative way when he called him "a stone cut by no human hand" (St. Justin Martyr, *Dialogue with Trypho* 76). The one described in Nebuchadnezzar's dream as a rock hewn without hands is now presented as the son of man, foreshadowing the Son of God, who takes to himself human flesh (St. Jerome, *Commentary on Daniel* 7, 13–14).

7:14 shall not be destroyed: A similar statement appears in 2:44, indicating that the kingdom of God foreseen by Nebuchadnezzar is none other than the kingdom of the "son of man" (7:13).

---

*7:8, *another horn, a little one*: Antiochus Epiphanes, who originally was of no importance.
†7:13, a *son of man*: The same title with which God addressed Ezekiel. Here it means someone who is more than human.

Daniel's Visions Interpreted

15 "As for me, Daniel, my spirit within me was anxious and the visions of my head alarmed me. [16]I approached one of those who stood there and asked him the truth concerning all this. So he told me, and made known to me the interpretation of the things. [17]'These four great beasts are four kings who shall arise out of the earth. [18]But the saints of the Most High shall receive the kingdom, and possess the kingdom for ever, for ever and ever.'

19 "Then I desired to know the truth concerning the fourth beast, which was different from all the rest, exceedingly terrifying, with its teeth of iron and claws of bronze; and which devoured and broke in pieces, and stamped the residue with its feet; [20]and concerning the ten horns that were on its head, and the other horn which came up and before which three of them fell, the horn which had eyes and a mouth that spoke great things, and which seemed greater than its fellows. [21]As I looked, this horn made war with the saints, and prevailed over them, [22]until the Ancient of Days came, and judgment was given for the saints of the Most High, and the time came when the saints received the kingdom.

[23]"Thus he said: 'As for the fourth beast,
there shall be a fourth kingdom on earth,
    which shall be different from all the kingdoms,
and it shall devour the whole earth,
    and trample it down, and break it to
        pieces.
[24]As for the ten horns,
out of this kingdom
    ten kings shall arise,
    and another shall arise after them;
he shall be different from the former ones,
    and shall put down three kings.

[25]He shall speak words against the Most High,
    and shall wear out the saints of the Most High,
    and shall think to change the times and the
        law;
and they shall be given into his hand
    for a time, two times, and half a time.
[26]But the court shall sit in judgment,
    and his dominion shall be taken away,
    to be consumed and destroyed to the end.
[27]And the kingdom and the dominion
    and the greatness of the kingdoms under the
        whole heaven
    shall be given to the people of the saints of the
        Most High;
their kingdom shall be an everlasting kingdom,
    and all dominions shall serve and obey them.'

28 "Here is the end of the matter. As for me, Daniel, my thoughts greatly alarmed me, and my color changed; but I kept the matter in my mind."

Vision of a Ram and a Goat

8 In the third year of the reign of King Belshaz'zar a vision appeared to me, Daniel, after that which appeared to me at the first. [2]And I saw in the vision; and when I saw, I was in Susa the capital, which is in the province of E'lam; and I saw in the vision, and I was at the river U'lai. [3]I raised my eyes and saw, and behold, a ram standing on the bank of the river. It had two horns; and both horns were high, but one was higher than the other, and the higher one came up last. [4]I saw the ram charging westward and northward and southward; no beast could stand before him, and there was no one who could rescue from his power; he did as he pleased and magnified himself.

5 As I was considering, behold, a he-goat came from the west across the face of the whole earth, without touching the ground; and the goat had a

---

7:20, 24: Rev 17:12.   **7:21:** Rev 13:7.   **7:25:** Rev 12:14.

7:16 one ... who stood: One of the angels standing before the Lord (7:10).

7:18 saints: Or, "holy ones", an expression that can refer to angels (Job 15:15; Zech 14:5) as well as the faithful of Israel (Ps 34:9; Wis 18:9). In Daniel's visions, it refers to Israel as a "people" (7:27) persecuted by earthly powers (7:21, 25; 8:24). Angels likewise figure in the judgment scene, but they are called "a thousand thousands" and "ten thousand times ten thousand" (7:10).

7:25 time ... times ... half a time: The time-unit in question is probably a year, in which case the expression means three and a half years (12:7). • In the Book of Revelation, this is the time frame in which Jerusalem and its sanctuary are laid waste (Rev 11:2) and the earliest Christian believers seek refuge outside the doomed city (Rev 12:14). Historically, the Jewish revolt that sparked the Roman conquest of Jerusalem lasted about three and a half years, from February of A.D. 67 until September of A.D. 70.

7:28 Here ... mind: The final verse written in Aramaic. The book continues in Hebrew from 8:1 to 12:13. See note on 2:4.

8:1 third year: Approximately 550 B.C., two years after Daniel's dream in chap. 7.

8:2–14 Daniel's second vision concerns the Medo-Persian empire (the ram, 8:20) and its conquest by the Greeks (the he-goat, 8:21). The goat's "conspicuous horn" is Alexander the Great (8:5), and the "four conspicuous horns" that replace him are the four generals who assumed control of Alexander's empire after his death in 323 B.C. (8:8). Finally, the "little horn" that comes later is Antiochus IV Epiphanes (8:9), the Seleucid king responsible for persecuting the Jews and desecrating the Jerusalem Temple in the second century B.C.

8:2 Susa: Former capital of the Medes and royal residence of later Persian kings (Esther 11:3). It lies over 200 miles east of Babylon in modern Iran. **Ulai:** A canal that connected the rivers Choaspes and Coprates near Susa.

8:3 one was higher: Recalls how the bear in Daniel's first vision was "raised up on one side" (7:5). Both images make the same point: Persia was the stronger and superior partner in the Medo-Persian union.

8:4 westward ... southward: The imperial expansion of the Medo-Persian empire over the eastern Mediterranean world.

8:5 from the west: Alexander and his armies swept over the Near East from his home in Macedon (northern Greece). **without touching the ground:** i.e., with incredible speed.

conspicuous horn between his eyes. [6]He came to the ram with the two horns, which I had seen standing on the bank of the river, and he ran at him in his mighty wrath. [7]I saw him come close to the ram, and he was enraged against him and struck the ram and broke his two horns; and the ram had no power to stand before him, but he cast him down to the ground and trampled upon him; and there was no one who could rescue the ram from his power. [8]Then the he-goat magnified himself exceedingly; but when he was strong, the great horn was broken, and instead of it there came up four conspicuous horns toward the four winds of heaven.

9 Out of one of them came forth a little horn, which grew exceedingly great toward the south, toward the east, and toward the glorious land. [10]It grew great, even to the host of heaven; and some of the host of the stars it cast down to the ground, and trampled upon them. [11]It magnified itself, even up to the Prince of the host; and the continual burnt offering was taken away from him, and the place of his sanctuary was overthrown. [12]And the host was given over to it together with the continual burnt offering through transgression;[n] and truth was cast down to the ground, and the horn acted and prospered. [13]Then I heard a holy one speaking; and another holy one said to the one that spoke, "For how long is the vision concerning the continual burnt offering, the transgression that makes desolate, and the giving over of the sanctuary and host to be trampled under foot?"[o] [14]And he said to him,[p] "For two thousand and three hundred evenings and

---

8:10: Rev 12:4.   **8:13:** Lk 21:24.

8:7 trampled upon: Medo-Persia was fully overrun by Greek conquerors by 323 B.C.

8:8 four conspicuous horns: Four generals who succeeded Alexander the Great and took control of various parts of his empire: Cassander (Macedonia, Greece), Lysimachus (Thrace, Asia Minor), Ptolemy (Egypt, Palestine, Cyprus), and Seleucis (Syria, Mesopotamia). These may be depicted in 7:6 as the four heads of the leopard.

8:9 the glorious land: The land of Israel.

8:10 even to ... heaven: Antiochus Epiphanes was a man of colossal arrogance and ego, here symbolized by the horn that exalts itself up to the stars (cf. Is 14:13). **the stars:** Represent the wise among God's people (12:3).

8:11 Prince of the host: Yahweh, often described in the Bible as "the Lord of hosts" (1 Sam 1:3; Ps 24:10; Is 6:3).

continual burnt offering: Refers to the twice-daily liturgy of the Temple, where a lamb was sacrificed along with incense, grain, and wine every morning and evening (Ex 29:38–42; Num 28:2–8). These and all sacrifices were halted by Antiochus' suppression of Judaism (1 Mac 1:44–45). **overthrown:** Antiochus seized control of the Jerusalem Temple for three years, from December 167 to December 164 B.C.

8:13 a holy one: An angel (4:13). **the transgression that makes desolate:** The erection of a pagan altar in the sanctuary at Jerusalem. Elsewhere this is called "the abomination that makes desolate" (11:31; 12:11). For details, see note on 11:31.

8:14 evenings and mornings: Perhaps 2,300 is the sum of evenings and mornings added together. It would thus refer to 1,150 days (= 3 years and 55 days), a close approximation to the three years that Antiochus Epiphanes desecrated Israel's sanctuary. See note on 8:11. **restored:** By the Maccabees, who cleansed and rededicated the Temple in 164 B.C. (1 Mac 4:36–58).

---

[n] Heb obscure.
[o] Heb obscure.
[p] Theodotion Gk Syr Vg: Heb *me*.

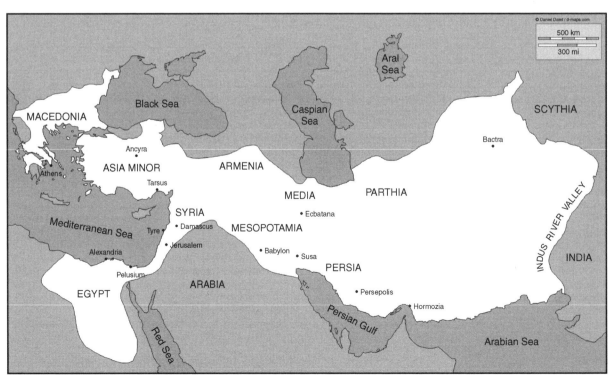

Extent of Alexander's Empire (323 B.C.)

mornings; then the sanctuary shall be restored to its rightful state."

Gabriel Interprets the Vision

15 When I, Daniel, had seen the vision, I sought to understand it; and behold, there stood before me one having the appearance of a man. [16]And I heard a man's voice between the banks of the U'lai, and it called, "Gabriel, make this man understand the vision." [17]So he came near where I stood; and when he came, I was frightened and fell upon my face. But he said to me, "Understand, O son of man, that the vision is for the time of the end."

18 As he was speaking to me, I fell into a deep sleep with my face to the ground; but he touched me and set me on my feet. [19]He said, "Behold, I will make known to you what shall be at the latter end of the indignation; for it pertains to the appointed time of the end. [20]As for the ram which you saw with the two horns, these are the kings of Me'dia and Persia. [21]And the he-goat[q] is the king of Greece; and the great horn between his eyes is the first king. [22]As for the horn that was broken, in place of which four others arose, four kingdoms shall arise from his[r] nation, but not with his power. [23]And at the latter end of their rule, when the transgressors have reached their full measure, a king of bold countenance, one who understands riddles, shall arise. [24]His power shall be great,[s] and he shall cause fearful destruction, and shall succeed in what he does, and destroy mighty men and the people of the saints. [25]By his cunning he shall make deceit prosper under his hand, and in his own mind he shall magnify himself. Without warning he shall destroy many; and he shall even rise up against the Prince of princes; but, by no human hand, he shall be broken. [26]The vision of the evenings and the mornings which has been told is true; but seal up the vision, for it pertains to many days hence."

27 And I, Daniel, was overcome and lay sick for some days; then I rose and went about the king's business; but I was appalled by the vision and did not understand it.

Daniel's Prayer for the People

9 In the first year of Dari'us the son of Ahas'uerus, by birth a Mede, who became king over the realm of the Chalde'ans— [2]in the first year of his reign, I, Daniel, perceived in the books the number of years which, according to the word of the Lord to Jeremi'ah the prophet, must pass before the end of the desolations of Jerusalem, namely, seventy years.

3 Then I turned my face to the Lord God, seeking him by prayer and supplications with fasting and sackcloth and ashes. [4]I prayed to the Lord my God and made confession, saying, "O Lord, the great and awesome God, who keeps covenant and merciful love with those who love him and keep his commandments, [5]we have sinned and done wrong and acted wickedly and rebelled, turning aside from your commandments and ordinances; [6]we have not listened to your servants the prophets, who spoke in your name to our kings, our princes, and our fathers, and to all the people of the land. [7]To you, O Lord, belongs righteousness, but to us confusion of face, as at this day, to the men of Judah, to the inhabitants of Jerusalem, and to all Israel, those that are near and those that are far away, in all the lands to which you have driven them, because of the treachery which they have committed against you. [8]To us, O Lord, belongs confusion of face, to our kings, to our princes, and to our fathers, because

---

8:15 appearance of a man: The archangel Gabriel, who is sent from heaven to interpret Daniel's vision (8:16; 9:21).

8:17 fell upon my face: A typical response to the overwhelming experience of coming face to face with God or one of his angels (Gen 17:3; Josh 5:14; Ezek 1:28; Rev 1:17) (CCC 330). **time of the end:** Not the end of history, but the end of Antiochus Epiphanes' assault on the Jewish way of life (1 Mac 1:29–61).

8:24 people of the saints: The faithful of Israel.

8:25 against the Prince: Indicates that Antiochus will assert himself against the Lord. This detail of the prophecy proved to be quite accurate, for the Seleucid king declared himself to be *theos epiphanēs*, "God Manifest". **no human hand:** Antiochus was brought low, not by the human hand of a soldier or assassin, but by the hand of God, who struck the king with excruciating afflictions in his body (2 Mac 9:5–12).

8:26 many days hence: The prophecy concerns events to come several centuries after Daniel's lifetime.

9:1 first year: 539 B.C. **Darius:** On his identity, see note on 5:31. **Ahasuerus:** A Hebrew form of the name Xerxes. **Chaldeans:** Babylonians. See note on 2:2.

9:2 the books: The prophetical books of the OT. **seventy years:** Jeremiah foretold that Judah would serve its Babylonian conquerors for 70 years (Jer 25:11), after which the Lord would bring his exiled people back to Israel (Jer 29:10). Just about 70 years elapsed between the first deportation to Babylon in 605 B.C. (1:1–4) and the decree of Cyrus II in 538 B.C. that allowed Jewish captives to return to their homeland (2 Chron 36:22–23).

9:3 sackcloth and ashes: Sackcloth was a coarse, hair-spun fabric worn next to the skin (1 Kings 21:27), and ashes were sprinkled on the head (2 Sam 13:19). Both are public acts of mourning and repentance.

9:4–19 Daniel's prayer is a confession of national sin and an appeal for restoration. He is aware that Israel's distress is the just result of its disloyalty to the Lord and his covenant, yet he petitions Yahweh to restore blessings to his disgraced people. Similar confessions are uttered by Azariah (*3:3–22 in italics*), Ezra (Ezra 9:6–15), and Nehemiah (Neh 9:6–37) (CCC 2635).

9:7 righteousness: Indicates that Yahweh has been faithful to his covenant obligations toward Israel (9:14). See word study: *Righteous* at Neh 9:8. **confusion of face:** An idiom for humiliation and disgrace. **all Israel:** i.e., the whole tribal family of Israel.

---

[q]Or *shaggy he-goat.*
[r]Theodotion Gk Vg: Heb *the.*
[s]Theodotion and Beatty papyrus of Gk: Heb repeats *but not with his power* from verse 22.

we have sinned against you. ⁹To the Lord our God belong mercy and forgiveness; because we have rebelled against him, ¹⁰and have not obeyed the voice of the LORD our God by following his laws, which he set before us by his servants the prophets. ¹¹All Israel has transgressed your law and turned aside, refusing to obey your voice. And the curse and oath which are written in the law of Moses the servant of God have been poured out upon us, because we have sinned against him. ¹²He has confirmed his words, which he spoke against us and against our rulers who ruled us, by bringing upon us a great calamity; for under the whole heaven there has not been done the like of what has been done against Jerusalem. ¹³As it is written in the law of Moses, all this calamity has come upon us, yet we have not entreated the favor of the LORD our God, turning from our iniquities and giving heed to your truth. ¹⁴Therefore the LORD has kept ready the calamity and has brought it upon us; for the LORD our God is righteous in all the works which he has done, and we have not obeyed his voice. ¹⁵And now, O Lord our God, who brought your people out of the land of Egypt with a mighty hand, and have made you a name, as at this day, we have sinned, we have done wickedly. ¹⁶O Lord, according to all your righteous acts, let your anger and your wrath turn away from your city Jerusalem, your holy hill; because for our sins, and for the iniquities of our fathers, Jerusalem and your people have become a byword among all who are round about us. ¹⁷Now therefore, O our God, listen to the prayer of your servant and to his supplications, and for your own sake, O Lord,ᵗ cause your face to shine upon your sanctuary, which is desolate. ¹⁸O my God, incline your ear and hear; open your eyes and behold our desolations, and the city which is called by your name; for we do not present our supplications before you on the ground of our righteousness, but on the ground of your great mercy. ¹⁹O LORD, hear; O LORD, forgive; O LORD, give heed and act; delay not, for your own sake, O my God, because your city and your people are called by your name."

The Seventy Weeks

20 While I was speaking and praying, confessing my sin and the sin of my people Israel, and presenting my supplication before the LORD my God for the holy hill of my God; ²¹while I was speaking in prayer, the man Gabriel, whom I had seen in the vision at the first, came to me in swift flight at the time of the evening sacrifice. ²²He cameᵘ and he said to me, "O Daniel, I have now come out to give you wisdom and understanding. ²³At the beginning of your supplications a word went forth, and I have come to tell it to you, for you are greatly beloved; therefore consider the word and understand the vision.

24 * "Seventy weeks of years are decreed concerning your people and your holy city, to

---

9:11 the curse: The most severe curse of the Deuteronomic covenant, which is expulsion from the land of Israel and exile among foreign nations (Deut 28:63–68). **oath:** Israel pledged by oath to accept the Deuteronomic covenant when the people repeatedly uttered "Amen" at the ratification liturgy (Deut 27:14–26).

9:12 against Jerusalem: A reference to 586 B.C., when the Babylonians devastated the holy city and its sanctuary (2 Kings 25:8–10).

9:20 the holy hill: Zion, the mountain of Jerusalem (Ps 2:6).

9:21 the man Gabriel: The angel Gabriel, who came to Daniel years earlier appearing as a man (8:15–16). **evening sacrifice:** Approximately 3 P.M., when a second round of daily sacrifices (lamb, incense, grain, wine) would have been offered in the Temple (Ex 29:38–42). Though the sanctuary was in ruins in Daniel's day, the prophet continues to follow the rhythms of Israel's liturgical life by praying toward Jerusalem at the set times of worship (6:10). • Times of sacrifice in the Temple are also times of prayer and supplication to the Lord (Ezra 9:5; Jud 9:1; Ps 141:2; Acts 10:1–4). A parallel example is Zechariah, father of John the Baptist, who will also be greeted by the angel Gabriel at the time of the daily Temple liturgy (Lk 1:8–13, 19). Just as Daniel is granted a vision of the messianic future (9:24–27), so Zechariah will hear that the time of messianic fulfillment is close at hand (Lk 1:14–17).

9:24–27 Daniel's prophecy of the 70 weeks. It is a timetable of God's plan for the future that includes the restoration of Jerusalem after exile, the coming of an anointed Messiah, and a second destruction of Jerusalem and its sanctuary. Several details of the oracle are difficult to interpret, and this has resulted in a variety of interpretations in both ancient and modern times. Most can be fitted into one of three categories. (1) *Messianic View.* The majority of scholars over the centuries interpret the prophecy as culminating in the first century A.D. with the coming of Jesus and the Roman destruction of Jerusalem. This view will be maintained below. (2) *Maccabean View.* Modern critical scholars, as well as a few figures from antiquity, place the end of the 70 weeks in the second century B.C. with the desecration of the Temple under Antiochus IV Epiphanes, an event that helped to spark the Maccabean revolt. Advocates of this view tend to read the numbers of the prophecy as rough approximations rather than precise calculations. (3) *Eschatological View.* Some theologians in early Christian times, along with modern Dispensationalists, read the text as a prophecy of Christ's Second Coming and the defeat of the Antichrist at the consummation of history. Proponents of this interpretation normally insert a parenthesis or gap into the timetable in order to stretch the prophecy into the last days. • None of the prophets speak as clearly about Christ as Daniel. Not only does he affirm his coming, a prediction common to other prophets, but he also indicates the time of his coming (St. Jerome, *Commentary on Daniel*, prologue).

9:24 Seventy weeks of years: Not a reinterpretation of Jeremiah's prophecy of 70 years of exile (9:2; Jer 25:11; 29:10), but a recalculation of the penitential period that Israel must undergo because of its failure to repent (9:13–16). In other words, Israel's spiritual condition necessitates an extension of suffering before God's mercy is poured out in full measure. This new revelation to Daniel was to

---

ᵗ Theodotion Vg Compare Syr: Heb *for the Lord's sake.*

ᵘ Gk Syr: Heb *made to understand.*

*9:24–27: Prophecy of the seventy weeks. The prophecy, made to encourage the Jews in time of persecution, looks to the future Messianic age in the time of the end; cf. 12:9. The seventy weeks are seventy seven-year periods, i.e., 490 years. But we can hardly take it as an exact historical period. Its immediate application seems to be to the period 170–163 B.C., i.e., from the beginning of the persecution of the Jews by Antiochus Epiphanes to the purification of the temple and the death of Antiochus.

finish the transgression, to put an end to sin, and to atone for iniquity, to bring in everlasting righteousness, to seal both vision and prophet, and to anoint a most holy place.ᵛ ²⁵Know therefore and understand that from the going forth of the word to restore and build Jerusalem to the coming of an anointed one, a prince, there shall be seven weeks. Then for sixty-two weeks it shall be

built again with squares and moat, but in a troubled time. ²⁶And after the sixty-two weeks, an anointed one shall be cut off, and shall have nothing; and the people of the prince who is to come shall destroy the city and the sanctuary. Itsʷ end shall come with a flood, and to the end there shall be war; desolations are decreed. ²⁷And he shall make a strong covenant with many for one week; and for half of the week

---

9:27: Dan 11:31; 12:11; Mt 24:15; Mk 13:14.

---

prepare Jewish exiles for the disappointing news that the end of the Babylonian Captivity would only be a small beginning; Israel's full restoration as envisioned by the prophets is the hope of future generations. • Multiplying the time of exile by seven has its explanation in Leviticus, where Moses warned that failure to repent in spite of the Lord's discipline would result in "sevenfold" judgment (Lev 26:18, 21, 24, 28). The seventy weeks is thus equivalent to ten Jubilee cycles, each lasting 49 years (Lev 25:8–12). **finish ... anoint:** Six blessings in store for the world by the end of the 70 weeks. • Several parallels are noticeable between Daniel 9 and Isaiah 53. Both delineate God's plan to take away human iniquity and replace it with a gift of righteousness (compare 9:24 with Is 53:5–6, 10–12). Likewise, in both oracles, this involves the messianic figure being "cut off" by death (compare 9:26 with Is 53:8).

9:25 restore and build: The first term denotes a recovery of political control and self-government in Jerusalem

ᵛOr *thing* or *one*.
ʷOr *his*.

Word Study

Weeks (9:24)

shabua‘ (Heb.): a "week" or "seven consecutive days" (Gen 29:27; Lev 12:5; Deut 16:9). There is nothing unusual about the term beyond the fact that biblical revelation establishes the week as a primary unit of time that culminates in a seventh day Sabbath (Gen 2:2–3; Ex 20:8–11). Nevertheless, use of the term in the Book of Daniel calls for special comment. When Daniel is given a timetable of "seventy weeks" in 9:24, most scholars agree that *shabua‘* is used symbolically rather than literally: the week in this case refers to "seven years" instead of the usual "seven days". Hence, the RSV translates "weeks of years" where the Hebrew simply says "weeks". The prophecy thus covers a total of 490 years (= 70 × 7 years), which is subdivided into 7 weeks (49 years), 62 weeks (434 years), and 1 week (7 years). Precedent for calculations based on the scale of one day = one year can be found in other prophetic pronouncements of the Bible. For example, in Num 14:34, the Israelites are condemned to wander in the wilderness for 40 years because they refused to seize control of Canaan after 40 days of spying out the land. Also, in Ezek 4:4–6, the prophet lies on the ground for 430 days to signify the 430 years of punishment that lay ahead for Israel. These and other factors support the interpretation of Daniel's prophecy as 70 "weeks of years" rather than merely 70 "weeks".

(1 Kings 20:34; 2 Kings 14:22); the second, a rebuilding of its physical infrastructure. Historically, these are related to the joint mission of Ezra and Nehemiah in the fifth century B.C., the former reestablishing the governance of Judah and Jerusalem on the basis of Torah (Ezra 7:25–26; 10:1–17) and the latter reconstructing the city's walls and gates (Neh 3–6). In light of this, the **going forth of the word** is best identified with the decree of Artaxerxes I given to Ezra in 457 B.C. (Ezra 7:11–26). Counting forward 490 years from this date, the 70th week of the prophecy extends over the seven years from A.D. 27 to 34, a historical window that encompasses the ministry of Jesus and the birth of the Christian Church. **anointed one:** A future prince designated in Hebrew as *mashiah* or "Messiah". In the NT, the anointing of Jesus is closely connected with the descent of the Spirit at his Baptism (Lk 3:22; 4:18; Acts 10:38; CCC 436, 695). **seven ... sixty-two:** The RSV, following the Masoretic Hebrew text, separates the first seven weeks of the prophecy from the following 62 weeks. The result is a distinction in time and identity between the "anointed one" in 9:25 and the "anointed one" in 9:26. However, ancient versions of this passage in Greek, Latin, and Syriac all read "seven weeks and sixty-two weeks" without a punctuation break in between. On this reading, only one "anointed one" is expected after the passing of 69 weeks. These variations make it difficult to ascertain the original intention of the text. **squares:** Public spaces used for religious gatherings, political assemblies, and juridical proceedings (2 Chron 32:6; Ezra 10:9; Jer 26:10–14). Resumption of community life in Jerusalem is thus envisioned. **moat:** Perhaps a defensive trench around the city.

9:26 cut off: Slain or cut down. **people of the prince:** Perhaps the kinsmen of the Messiah, called a "prince" in 9:25. Alternatively, one might think of the Romans under the emperor Vespasian, who destroyed Jerusalem in A.D. 70. The historian Josephus, who witnessed the fall of the city firsthand, links the desolation prophesied by Daniel with this catastrophe (*Antiquities* 10, 276). **a flood:** An overwhelming force of devastation. The same Hebrew term denotes unstoppable military might in 11:22.

9:27 strong covenant: Seemingly a reference to the New Covenant ratified by the Messiah (Lk 22:20). **sacrifice ... cease:** This and the events that follow are best understood as a *consequence* of the 70 weeks, not as their *climax*, which is linked rather with the coming and cutting off of the Messiah. In other words, the Mosaic system of sacrifice will disappear with the fall of Jerusalem, yet its purpose and efficacy had already ceased once the perfect sacrifice of Christ was offered (Heb 9:9–14; 10:1–18). This is signified in the Synoptic Gospels by the tearing of the Temple veil at the time of the Crucifixion (Mt 27:51; Mk 15:38; Lk 23:45) (CCC 1330, 2100). **wing of abominations:** The Hebrew *kanaph* generally means "wing" but can also refer to the "extremity" of something. Perhaps the idea is that abominations will reach an extreme degree at the devastation of Jerusalem. Josephus says as much in his eyewitness account (*War* 5, 442). For the relation between this event and the "abomination" noted in later chapters, see note on 11:31. **poured out on the desolator:** The judgment destined to fall on the conqueror and persecutor of God's people, described in 7:11 as the burning of the fourth beast.

he shall cause sacrifice and offering to cease; and upon the wing of abominations shall come one who makes desolate, until the decreed end is poured out on the desolator."

Daniel's Vision "for Days Yet to Come"

10 †In the third year of Cyrus king of Persia a word was revealed to Daniel, who was named Belteshaz′zar. And the word was true, and it was a great conflict. And he understood the word and had understanding of the vision.

2 In those days I, Daniel, was mourning for three weeks. ³I ate no delicacies, no meat or wine entered my mouth, nor did I anoint myself at all, for the full three weeks. ⁴On the twenty-fourth day of the first month, as I was standing on the bank of the great river, that is, the Tigris, ⁵I lifted up my eyes and looked, and behold, a man clothed in linen, whose loins were belted with gold of U′phaz. ⁶His body was like beryl, his face like the appearance of lightning, his eyes like flaming torches, his arms and legs like the gleam of burnished bronze, and the sound of his words like the noise of a multitude. ⁷And I, Daniel, alone saw the vision, for the men who were with me did not see the vision, but a great trembling fell upon them, and they fled to hide themselves. ⁸So I was left alone and saw this great vision, and no strength was left in me; my radiant appearance was fearfully changed, and I retained no strength. ⁹Then I heard the sound of his words; and when I heard the sound of his words, I fell on my face in a deep sleep with my face to the ground.

10 And behold, a hand touched me and set me trembling on my hands and knees. ¹¹And he said to me, "O Daniel, man greatly beloved, give heed to the words that I speak to you, and stand upright, for now I have been sent to you." While he was speaking this word to me, I stood up trembling. ¹²Then he said to me, "Fear not, Daniel, for from the first day that you set your mind to understand and humbled yourself before your God, your words have been heard, and I have come because of your words. ¹³The prince of the kingdom of Persia withstood me twenty-one days; but Michael, one of the chief princes, came to help me, so I left him there with the prince of the kingdom of Persia* ¹⁴and came to make you understand what is to befall your people in the latter days. For the vision is for days yet to come."

15 When he had spoken to me according to these words, I turned my face toward the ground and was speechless. ¹⁶And behold, one in the likeness of the sons of men touched my lips; then I opened my mouth and spoke. I said to him who stood before me, "O my lord, by reason of the vision pains have come upon me, and I retain no strength. ¹⁷How can my lord's servant talk with my lord? For now no strength remains in me, and no breath is left in me."

18 Again one having the appearance of a man touched me and strengthened me. ¹⁹And he said,

---

10:5–6: Rev 1:13–14; 2:18. **10:13, 21:** Rev 12:7.

10:1—12:13 Daniel's fourth and final vision encompasses chaps. 10–12. Its focus is the Medo-Persian and Greek kingdoms, beginning with Cyrus II of Persia (559 to 530 B.C.) and followed by the tyrannical regime of the Seleucid ruler Antiochus IV Epiphanes (175 to 164 B.C.). Parts of the vision may be said to foreshadow messianic events already described in Daniel 9. Also, Christian tradition has frequently seen Antiochus as a type of the Antichrist to come. See notes on 11:21–45 and 11:31.

10:1 third year: 537 B.C., the third year since Cyrus II conquered Babylon and claimed it for Medo-Persia. **conflict:** The vision concerns opposition between angels (10:12–21) and nations (11:2–45).

10:3 no meat or wine: See note on 1:8. **anoint:** Anointing the head with oil was reserved for special or festive occasions (Ruth 3:3; Ps 23:5; 45:7).

10:4 first month: The springtime month of Nisan, corresponding to March-April.

10:5 a man clothed in linen: An angel from heaven clad in a priestly vestment (Lev 16:4; Ezek 9:2; Rev 15:6).

10:6 beryl: A translucent gold gemstone.

10:9 fell on my face: On this reaction, see note on 8:17.

10:12 humbled ... heard: In biblical teaching, the prayer of the humble reaches to heaven (Sir 35:17), but God opposes the proud (Prov 3:34; Jas 4:3–6; 1 Pet 5:5) (CCC 2559).

10:13 prince: An angel who has spiritual oversight and influence over an earthly nation. Reference is made in Daniel to the angelic patrons of Persia (10:13), Greece (10:20), and Israel (12:1). Jewish tradition traces this idea to the Greek LXX translation of Deut 32:8, which states that nations are divided "according to the number of the angels of God" (Deut 32:8 LXX). Christian tradition also teaches that God exercises his providential government over nations through the ministry of angels. They serve as helpers and protectors who are tasked with preserving some knowledge of God and his truth among those who are ignorant of supernatural revelation (e.g., St. Clement of Alexandria, *Stromata* 7, 2; St. Basil, *Against Eunomius* 3, 1). **withstood me:** The nature of the opposition is not specified. • Divine judgments relating to kingdoms and peoples are carried out by angels, whose actions are ruled by divine decree. But when kingdoms and peoples have contrary merits and demerits, so that one of these kingdoms or peoples is ruled over by another, this is a matter of divine wisdom that angels cannot know unless God reveals it to them. Angels are said to resist one another inasmuch as they consult God's will about contrary merits. Their wills are not in opposition, only the matters about which they seek knowledge (St. Thomas Aquinas, *Summa Theologiae* 1, 113, 8). **twenty-one days:** Another way of counting Daniel's "three weeks" of prayer and petition (10:2–3). **Michael:** The guardian angel of Israel (10:21; 12:1). His name in Hebrew means "Who is like God?" Michael is an archangel (Jude 9) who battles against Satan on behalf of the Lord and his people (Rev 12:7–9). Besides him, two other angels are identified by name in the Bible: Gabriel (8:16; Lk 1:19) and Raphael (Tob 5:4) (CCC 335).

10:14 days yet to come: The prophecy concerns events that would occur several centuries after Daniel's lifetime.

10:16 touched my lips: Suggests the prophet is spiritually cleansed and empowered for his mission (Is 6:7; Jer 1:9).

---

* Theodotion Compare Gk: Heb *I was left there with the kings of Persia*.
† 10–12: Summary of the history of the Persian and Greek periods down to Antiochus Epiphanes and thence to the time of the end.

"O man greatly beloved, fear not, peace be with you; be strong and of good courage." And when he spoke to me, I was strengthened and said, "Let my lord speak, for you have strengthened me." ²⁰Then he said, "Do you know why I have come to you? But now I will return to fight against the prince of Persia; and when I am through with him, behold, the prince of Greece will come. ²¹But I will tell you what is inscribed in the book of truth: there is none who contends by my side against these except Michael, your prince.

11 And as for me, in the first year of Dari′us the Mede, I stood up to confirm and strengthen him.

Coming Conflict of the Nations

2 "And now I will show you the truth. Behold, three more kings shall arise in Persia; and a fourth shall be far richer than all of them; and when he has become strong through his riches, he shall stir up all against the kingdom of Greece. ³Then a mighty king shall arise, who shall rule with great dominion and do according to his will. ⁴And when he has arisen, his kingdom shall be broken and divided toward the four winds of heaven, but not to his posterity, nor according to the dominion with which he ruled; for his kingdom shall be plucked up and go to others besides these.

5 "Then the king of the south shall be strong, but one of his princes shall be stronger than he and his dominion shall be a great dominion. ⁶After some years they shall make an alliance, and the daughter of the king of the south shall come to the king of the north to make peace; but she shall not retain the strength of her arm, and he and his offspring shall not endure; but she shall be given up, and her attendants, her child, and he who got possession ofʸ her.

7 "In those times a branchᶻ from her roots shall arise in his place; he shall come against the army and enter the fortress of the king of the north, and he shall deal with them and shall prevail. ⁸He shall also carry off to Egypt their gods with their molten images and with their precious vessels of silver and of gold; and for some years he shall refrain from attacking the king of the north. ⁹Then the latter shall come into the realm of the king of the south but shall return into his own land.

10 "His sons shall wage war and assemble a multitude of great forces, which shall come on and overflow and pass through, and again shall carry the war as far as his fortress. ¹¹Then the king of the south, moved with anger, shall come out and fight with the king of the north; and he shall raise a great multitude, but it shall be given into his hand. ¹²And when the multitude is taken, his heart shall be exalted, and he shall cast down tens of thousands, but he shall not prevail. ¹³For the king of the north shall again raise a multitude, greater than the

---

10:20 Persia . . . Greece: Successive empires of the biblical world, both of which assumed control over Israel in the postexilic period. Persian dominance lasted from 539 until about 331 B.C., and Greek dominance lasted from about 331 until 63 B.C.

11:1 first year: 539 B.C. The passage is best read as the final verse of chap. 10 rather than the first verse of chap. 11. **Darius:** On his identity, see note on 5:31.

11:2–4 The succession of the Medo-Persian empire by the Greek empire.

11:2 fourth: Xerxes I, king of Persia from 486 to 465 B.C. He launched an ill-fated invasion of Greece that ended with his defeat at the Battle of Salamis in 480 B.C.

11:3 mighty king: Alexander the Great, conqueror of the Persian kingdom. After his death in 323 B.C., his vast empire was divided up among four of his generals. His dominion was thus inherited, not by his "posterity", but by "others" who were not his sons (11:4). See note on 8:8.

11:5–20 Envisions a long-standing conflict between two of the Greek states: the Ptolemaic dynasty of Egypt and the Seleucid dynasty of Syria. Palestine was caught between these two rivals, being subject to Ptolemaic (ca. 270 to 198 B.C.) and then Seleucid rule (ca. 198 to 142 B.C.). Israel is the geographical center of the prophecy, which means the "kings of the north" are Seleucid monarchs and the "kings of the south" are Ptolemaic monarchs.

11:5 king of the south: Ptolemy I Soter (305 to 283 B.C.). **one of his princes:** Seleucus I Nicator (312 to 281 B.C.).

11:6 alliance: The treaty of 252 B.C., when the Ptolemaic princess, Berenice, daughter of Ptolemy II Philadelphus (285 to 246 B.C.), was given in marriage to Antiochus II Theos of Syria (261 to 246 B.C.).

11:7 a branch: Ptolemy III Euergetes, brother of Berenice (246 to 221 B.C.). **the fortress:** The Syrian city of Antioch.

11:8 king of the north: Seleucus II Callinicus (246 to 226 B.C.).

11:11–12 Antiochus III the Great of Syria (223 to 187 B.C.) tries but fails to wrest control of Palestine from Ptolemy IV Philopator of Egypt (221 to 203 B.C.).

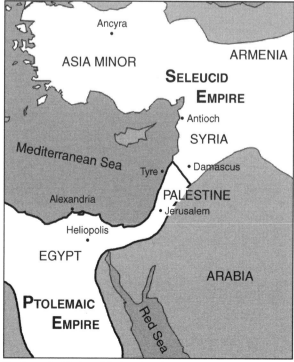

Ptolemaic Rule of Palestine (270–198 B.C.)

ʸ Or *supported.*
ᶻ Gk: Heb *from a branch.*

former; and after some years[a] he shall come on with a great army and abundant supplies.

14 "In those times many shall rise against the king of the south; and the men of violence among your own people shall lift themselves up in order to fulfil the vision; but they shall fail. [15]Then the king of the north shall come and throw up siegeworks, and take a well-fortified city. And the forces of the south shall not stand, or even his picked troops, for there shall be no strength to stand. [16]But he who comes against him shall do according to his own will, and none shall stand before him; and he shall stand in the glorious land, and all of it shall be in his power. [17]He shall set his face to come with the strength of his whole kingdom, and he shall bring terms of peace[b] and perform them. He shall give him the daughter of women to destroy the kingdom;[c] but it shall not stand or be to his advantage. [18]Afterward he shall turn his face to the islands, and shall take many of them; but a commander shall put an end to his insolence; indeed[d] he shall turn his insolence back upon him. [19]Then he shall turn his face back toward the fortresses of his own land; but he shall stumble and fall, and shall not be found.

20 "Then shall arise in his place one who shall send an exactor of tribute through the glory of the kingdom; but within a few days he shall be broken, neither in anger nor in battle. [21]In his place shall arise a contemptible person to whom royal majesty has not been given; he shall come in without warning and obtain the kingdom by flatteries. [22]Armies shall be utterly swept away before him and broken, and the prince of the covenant also. [23]And from the time that an alliance is made with him he shall act deceitfully; and he shall become strong with a small people. [24]Without warning he shall come into the richest parts[e] of the province; and he shall do what neither his fathers nor his fathers' fathers have done, scattering among them plunder, spoil, and goods. He shall devise plans against strongholds, but only for a time. [25]And he shall stir up his power and his courage against the king of the south with a great army; and the king of the south shall wage war with an exceedingly great and mighty army; but he shall not stand, for plots shall be devised against him. [26]Even those who eat his rich food shall be his undoing; his army shall be swept away, and many shall fall down slain. [27]And as for the two

---

11:14 king of the south: Ptolemy V Epiphanes (203 to 181 B.C.). **men of violence:** Jewish revolutionaries who sided with the Seleucids but were unsuccessful in throwing off the yoke of Ptolemaic rule.

11:15–16 Antiochus III finally succeeds in defeating his Ptolemaic rival at the battle of Paneas and bringing Palestine under Seleucid control (ca. 198 B.C.).

11:15 well-fortified city: Sidon, on the Mediterranean coast of Phoenicia.

11:16 the glorious land: The land of Israel.

11:17 daughter of women: Seleucid princess Cleopatra I, given in marriage to Ptolemy V in order to cement a political alliance between Egypt and Syria around 194 B.C.

11:18 a commander: Lucius Cornelius Scipio, who in 190 B.C. led Roman forces to victory over Antiochus III at Magnesia in Asia Minor.

11:19 stumble and fall: Antiochus III died in 187 B.C. after attempting to loot the temple of Bel at Elymais.

11:20 exactor of tribute: Heliodorus, sent to Jerusalem by Seleucus IV Philopator in 175 B.C. to confiscate the funds in the Temple treasury (2 Mac 3:7–40).

✚ **11:21–45** The reign of Antiochus IV Epiphanes, here called a **contemptible person** (11:21). History remembers him as the villain who ruthlessly imposed Greek culture on Palestine and outlawed the practice of Judaism (1 Mac 1:10–61). He usurped the Seleucid throne in 175 B.C. by out-maneuvering its rightful heir, his nephew Demetrius I; then in December of 167 B.C., he marched on Jerusalem, massacred thousands, and defiled the Temple (2 Mac 5:11–20). Not content with political or military glory, he made audacious claims to divinity (11:36–37). Antiochus' reign of terror finally ended with his death in 164 B.C. • Early Christian tradition, noting that several details in these verses seem to disagree with other sources, or else have no known link with the historical career of Antiochus, often considered this tyrant a prefiguration of the future Antichrist. Daniel's prediction of

events in the second century B.C. is thus said to blend with prophetic statements about the end times, although opinions differ over which details relate to this more distant future. In any case, mention of the general resurrection in 12:2 shows that the scope of Daniel's final vision stretches far beyond Hellenistic and Roman times to the consummation of history itself (CCC 675–76).

11:22 prince of the covenant: Probably Onias III, the Jewish high priest who was deposed in 175 and then murdered in 171 B.C. (2 Mac 4:34–35).

11:25 against ... the south: Antiochus IV launched his first invasion of Egypt in 170 B.C. (1 Mac 1:16–19).

Seleucid Rule of Palestine (198–142 B.C.)

---

[a] Heb *at the end of the times years.*

[b] Gk: Heb *upright ones.*

[c] Heb *her* or *it.*

[d] Heb obscure.

[e] Or *among the richest men.*

kings, their minds shall be bent on mischief; they shall speak lies at the same table, but to no avail; for the end is yet to be at the time appointed. ²⁸And he shall return to his land with great substance, but his heart shall be set against the holy covenant. And he shall work his will, and return to his own land.

29 "At the time appointed he shall return and come into the south; but it shall not be this time as it was before. ³⁰For ships of Kittim shall come against him, and he shall be afraid and withdraw, and shall turn back and be enraged and take action against the holy covenant. He shall turn back and give heed to those who forsake the holy covenant. ³¹Forces from him shall appear and profane the temple and fortress, and shall take away the continual burnt offering. And they shall set up the abomination that makes desolate. ³²He shall seduce with flattery those who violate the covenant; but the people who know their God shall stand firm and take action. ³³And those among the people who are wise shall make many understand, though they shall fall by sword and flame, by captivity and plunder, for some days. ³⁴When they fall, they shall receive a little help. And many shall join themselves to them with flattery; ³⁵and some of those who are wise shall fall, to refine and to cleanse them ᶠ and to make them white, until the time of the end, for it is yet for the time appointed.

36 "And the king shall do according to his will; he shall exalt himself and magnify himself above every god, and shall speak astonishing things against the God of gods. He shall prosper till the indignation is accomplished; for what is determined shall be done. ³⁷He shall give no heed to the gods of his fathers, or to the one beloved by women; he shall not give heed to any other god, for he shall magnify himself above all. ³⁸He shall honor the god of fortresses instead of these; a god whom his fathers did not know he shall honor with gold and silver, with precious stones and costly gifts. ³⁹He shall deal with the strongest fortresses by the help of a foreign god; those who acknowledge him he shall magnify with honor. He shall make them rulers over many and shall divide the land for a price.

The Time of the End

40 "At the time of the end the king of the south shall attack ᵍ him; but the king of the north shall rush upon him like a whirlwind, with chariots and horsemen, and with many ships; and he shall come into countries and shall overflow and pass through. ⁴¹He shall come into the glorious land. And tens of thousands shall fall, but these shall be delivered out of his hand: E'dom and Moab and the main part of the Am'monites. ⁴²He shall stretch out his hand against the countries, and the land of Egypt shall not escape. ⁴³He shall become ruler of the treasures

---

11:31: Dan 9:27; 12:11; Mt 24:15; Mk 13:14.   **11:36:** Ezek 28:2; 2 Thess 2:4; Rev 13:5.

11:28 against the holy covenant: Against the religion of Judaism. In ca. 169 B.C., Antiochus plundered the Jerusalem Temple of its sacred monies and furnishings and took them back to Syria (1 Mac 1:20–24).

11:30 Kittim: Hebrew name for peoples that come from Cyprus as well as other islands and coastlands of the Mediterranean (Num 24:24). In the Greek LXX version of this verse, and several times in the Dead Sea Scrolls, the Kittim are identified as the Romans. **afraid and withdraw:** Antiochus IV initiated a second offensive against Egypt in 168 B.C. However, when confronted by a Roman delegation outside the city of Alexandria, he chose to retreat rather than face the military might of Rome. **those who forsook:** Apostate Jews who agreed to implement the Hellenizing policies of Antiochus IV (1 Mac 1:11–15).

11:31 continual burnt offering: The morning and evening sacrifices of the Temple suppressed by Antiochus IV (1 Mac 1:45). See note on 8:11. **the abomination that makes desolate:** Rendered "abomination of desolation" in the Greek LXX. It refers to a pagan altar dedicated to the Greek god Zeus Olympios that Antiochus Epiphanes erected in the Temple at Jerusalem in 167 B.C. (2 Mac 6:1–2) and used for sacrifices of swine (Josephus, *Antiquities* 12, 253). This was his most outrageous insult to the Jewish religion. The sanctuary remained desecrated by the abomination for three full years, at the end of which it was cleansed and rededicated by Judas Maccabeus (1 Mac 4:36–59; 2 Mac 10:1–8). At another level, a case can be made that Daniel's prophecy presupposes a typological view of history in which evil manifests itself in a recurring pattern. Looking backward, the desolation caused by Antiochus in the second century B.C. recapitulates the "desolate" state of the sanctuary left

by conquering Babylonians in the sixth century B.C. Looking forward, his actions anticipate an event in messianic times when the city and sanctuary of Jerusalem will again be laid waste (9:26) by "one who makes desolate" (9:27). • Jesus uses the same language to prophesy the Roman destruction of Jerusalem that took place in A.D. 70. He speaks of a "desolating sacrilege" that recalls the abomination of Antiochus and results once again in a pagan desecration of the Temple (Mt 24:15; Mk 13:14; cf. Lk 21:20) (CCC 585).

11:33 who are wise: The faithful remnant of Israel, many of whom gave their lives as martyrs during Antiochus' persecution (11:34–35; 1 Mac 1:63; 2 Mac 7:1–42) (CCC 2473).

11:34 a little help: Alludes to the Maccabees and their modest band of supporters, who took up arms against the Seleucid oppressors. The comment is sometimes taken to mean that the visionary considered a military response to Jewish persecution ineffective and/or inappropriate.

11:35 refine … cleanse: Here and elsewhere Scripture reveals that spiritual benefits can come through suffering and martyrdom (Rev 7:14).

11:36 above every god: Antiochus IV made arrogant claims to divinity on his coins, which listed his title as *theos epiphanēs*, "God Manifest". • Paul borrows language from this passage when he describes the Antichrist of the last days. Like Antiochus, this dreaded figure will exalt "himself against every so-called god" and proclaim himself "to be God" (2 Thess 2:4).

11:37 gods of his fathers: Such as the Greek god Apollos, whose importance may have diminished with Antiochus' heightened concern to venerate Zeus. **one beloved by women:** Possibly a reference to Tammuz, also called Adonis, a vegetation god revered by many women in the Near Eastern world (Ezek 8:14).

11:38 god of fortresses: Often identified as Jupiter Capitolinus.

ᶠ Gk: Heb *among them.*
ᵍ Heb *thrust at.*

of gold and of silver, and all the precious things of Egypt; and the Libyans and the Ethiopians shall follow in his train. [44]But tidings from the east and the north shall alarm him, and he shall go forth with great fury to exterminate and utterly destroy many. [45]And he shall pitch his palatial tents between the sea and the glorious holy mountain; yet he shall come to his end, with none to help him.

The Resurrection of the Dead

12 "At that time shall arise Michael, the great prince who has charge of your people. And there shall be a time of trouble, such as never has been since there was a nation till that time; but at that time your people shall be delivered, every one whose name shall be found written in the book. [2]And many of those who sleep in the dust of the earth shall awake, some to everlasting life, and some to shame and everlasting contempt. [3]And those who are wise shall shine like the brightness of the firmament; and those who turn many to righteousness, like the stars for ever and ever. [4]But you, Daniel, shut up the words, and seal the book, until the time of the end.

Many shall run back and forth, and knowledge shall increase."

5 Then I Daniel looked, and behold, two others stood, one on this bank of the stream and one on that bank of the stream. [6]And I[h] said to the man clothed in linen, who was above the waters of the stream, "How long shall it be till the end of these wonders?" [7]The man clothed in linen, who was above the waters of the stream, raised his right hand and his left hand toward heaven; and I heard him swear by him who lives for ever that it would be for a time, two times, and half a time; and that when the shattering of the power of the holy people comes to an end all these things would be accomplished. [8]I heard, but I did not understand. Then I said, "O my lord, what shall be the issue of these things?" [9]He said, "Go your way, Daniel, for the words are shut up and sealed until the time of the end. [10]Many shall purify themselves, and make themselves white, and be refined; but the wicked shall do wickedly; and none of the wicked shall understand; but those who are wise shall

---

12:1: Mt 24:21; Mk 13:19; Rev 12:7; 16:18.   **12:2:** Mt 25:46.   **12:3:** Mt 13:43.
12:4: Rev 22:10.   **12:7:** Rev 4:9; 10:5; 12:14.

11:44 tidings ... east ... north: Possibly reports of insurrection among the Parthians and Armenians.

11:45 palatial: Translates a Persian loanword meaning "palace". Here it seems to mean a tentlike "pavilion" pitched in a war camp. **the sea:** The Mediterranean. **the glorious holy mountain:** The Temple Mount in Jerusalem. **shall come to his end:** Prophesies the death of Antiochus in 164 B.C. Daniel's description, which seems to imply that Antiochus will perish while staging a military offensive in Israel, is quite different from that of the Greek historian Polybius, who states that Antiochus met his demise after an unsuccessful attempt to rob the temple of Artemis in Persia (*Histories* 31, 9). A few considerations may be offered in view of this apparent historical error. (1) Perhaps the prophecy is worded to evoke the fate of Gog, another invader from the north, who is slain in the land of Israel and buried "east of the sea" (Ezek 39:11). The effect would be to classify Antiochus among the archenemies of God whose downfall is assured by Scripture. (2) Perhaps the point of the vision is to indicate the reason *why* Antiochus comes to grief rather than the whereabouts of his death. According to the Books of Maccabees, the death of Antiochus was a divine punishment for his savage assaults on Jerusalem, both accomplished (1 Mac 6:1–16) and intended (2 Mac 9:1–29). A similar message may be conveyed here. (3) Another possibility, maintained by those who relate the vision to the distant future, is that 11:45 actually describes the death of the Antichrist, who is thought to be modeled on the figure of Antiochus Epiphanes.

12:1–5 Suffering and salvation await Israel after Daniel's lifetime. Despite the tribulation to come, readers can know that a resurrection of the dead and a general judgment are certain. Those who remain faithful, even unto death, are thereby assured of the blessings that the messianic kingdom of God will bring (7:18).

12:1 At that time: i.e., at the time of the end (11:40), which culminates with the demise of Antiochus IV (11:45). **Michael:** The guardian angel of Israel. See note on 10:13. **the book:** Not an actual registry of names that exists in heaven,

but an image that symbolizes God's knowledge of the saints destined for his blessings (Ex 32:32; Ps 69:28; Is 4:3; Lk 10:20).

12:2 sleep: A euphemism for death (1 Cor 15:20), which entails a return of the body to the dust of the ground (Gen 3:19; Eccles 12:7). **awake:** The dead will be raised up to a new and everlasting existence (Is 26:19). **life ... shame:** Separate destinies are allotted to the wise and the wicked in the afterlife. Significantly, this is one of the first passages in the Bible that envisions a general resurrection of saints and sinners alike; hereafter it would become a widely accepted doctrine in both Jewish and Christian theology (Jn 5:28–29; Acts 24:15). Historically, belief in a bodily resurrection was directly relevant to Jews facing martyrdom at the hands of Antiochus Epiphanes. Scripture makes this clear in the case of the seven brothers who accept torture and death in the hope that God will raise them again to new life (2 Mac 7:1–40) (CCC 992, 998).

12:3 wise shall shine: A promise that the faithful of Israel will be glorified. They will join the company of angels—luminous spirits that Jewish tradition associated with the stars of the night sky (Judg 5:20; Job 38:7; Rev 1:20).

12:4 seal the book: Wax seals were placed along the vertical edge of a rolled-up scroll to prevent it from unraveling. Daniel is to seal up the written account of his visions because they concern events scheduled to occur long after his lifetime (8:26; 10:14).

12:5 two others: Presumably angels.

12:6 man clothed in linen: The angel sent to reveal the future to Daniel in his final vision (10:5–6).

12:7 raised his right hand: Raising the hand was a symbolic oath gesture in the biblical world (Deut 32:40; Rev 10:5–6). **swear by him:** The oath is sworn by invoking the name of God and calling on him to act as the divine Witness and Enforcer of the pledge being made. **time ... times ... half a time:** Three and a half years, the approximate duration of Antiochus Epiphanes' assault on Palestinian Judaism. For a different application, see note on 7:25. **all these things:** The events prophesied in the final vision (chaps. 10–12).

12:10 purify themselves: The spiritual effect of martyrdom (11:35; Rev 6:9–11; 7:14).

---

[h] Gk Vg: Heb *he*.

understand. [11]And from the time that the continual burnt offering is taken away, and the abomination that makes desolate is set up, there shall be a thousand two hundred and ninety days. [12]Blessed is he who waits and comes to the thousand three hundred and thirty-five days. [13]But go your way till the end; and you shall rest, and shall stand in your allotted place at the end of the days."

Two Elders' Lust for Susanna

13 *There was a man living in Babylon whose name was Jo'akim. [2]And he took a wife named Susanna, the daughter of Hilki'ah, a very beautiful woman and one who feared the Lord. [3]Her parents were righteous, and had taught their daughter according to the law of Moses. [4]Jo'akim was very rich, and had a spacious garden adjoining his house; and the Jews used to come to him because he was the most honored of them all.

5 In that year two elders from the people were appointed as judges. Concerning them the Lord had said: "Iniquity came forth from Babylon, from elders who were judges, who were supposed to govern the people." [6]These men were frequently at Jo'akim's house, and all who had suits at law came to them.

7 When the people departed at noon, Susanna would go into her husband's garden to walk. [8]The two elders used to see her every day, going in and walking about, and they began to desire her. [9]And they perverted their minds and turned away their eyes from looking to Heaven or remembering righteous judgments. [10]Both were overwhelmed with passion for her, but they did not tell each other

of their distress, [11]for they were ashamed to disclose their lustful desire to possess her. [12]And they watched eagerly, day after day, to see her.

13 They said to each other, "Let us go home, for it is mealtime." [14]And when they went out, they parted from each other. But turning back, they met again; and when each pressed the other for the reason, they confessed their lust. And then together they arranged for a time when they could find her alone.

The Elders Attempt to Seduce Susanna

15 Once, while they were watching for an opportune day, she went in as before with only two maids, and wished to bathe in the garden, for it was very hot. [16]And no one was there except the two elders, who had hid themselves and were watching her. [17]She said to her maids, "Bring me oil and ointments, and shut the garden doors so that I may bathe." [18]They did as she said, shut the garden doors, and went out by the side doors to bring what they had been commanded; and they did not see the elders, because they were hidden.

19 When the maids had gone out, the two elders rose and ran to her, and said: [20]"Look, the garden doors are shut, no one sees us, and we are in love with you; so give your consent, and lie with us. [21]If you refuse, we will testify against you that a young man was with you, and this was why you sent your maids away."

22 Susanna sighed deeply, and said, "I am hemmed in on every side. For if I do this thing, it is death for me; and if I do not, I shall not escape

---

12:11: Dan 9:27; 11:31; Mt 24:15; Mk 13:14.

12:11–12 The persecution of Antiochus Epiphanes is still in view. However, it is unclear what distinguishes the different time calculations associated with it in 8:14 (1150 days), 12:7 (3½ years = 1260 days), 12:11 (1290 days), and 12:12 (1335 days). Perhaps they measure different aspects of the Seleucid persecution that stretched beyond the three years of the Temple's desecration from 167 to 164 B.C.

13:1—14:42 Chaps. 13 and 14 survive only in Greek translations of the OT, but it is probable they were originally written in Hebrew or Aramaic. • Neither chapter is included in the biblical canon accepted by rabbinic Judaism and historic Protestantism, but the Catholic Church considers them fully inspired and canonical texts of Scripture (Council of Trent, session 4, decree 1).

13:1–64 The story of Susanna. In the Greek version translated here (Θ), the story stands at the beginning rather than at the end of the Book of Daniel, perhaps because Daniel appears as a "young lad" (13:45). Its placement after chap. 12 follows the order of the Greek LXX and Latin Vulgate.

13:1 Joakim: The name in Hebrew means "Yahweh will establish". He is described as a wealthy and influential patriarch of the Jewish Diaspora in Babylon, though he plays no active role in the narrative.

13:2 Susanna: The name in Hebrew means "lily", a flower symbolic of feminine beauty (Song 2:2). She is remembered

for being exceptionally attractive (Dan 13:31), pious (13:35), and chaste (13:23). **Hilkiah:** The name in Hebrew means "Yahweh is my portion."

13:5 two elders: The unnamed villains of the story. Their role as corrupt leaders (13:52–53) and shameless womanizers (13:56–57) brings to mind Hophni and Phinehas, the wicked sons of Eli (1 Sam 2:12–17, 22). **Iniquity came forth:** The source of the quotation is unknown.

13:9 Heaven: A Jewish expression for "God" (4:26; 1 Mac 3:18–19; 4:10).

13:12 they watched: The men are mastered by lust. Instead of diverting their gaze from Susanna, they stoke their illicit passions by feasting their eyes on her physical beauty (13:32).

13:17 maids: Female attendants would not be out of place in a wealthy household such as Susanna's. **oil:** Applied as a cosmetic (Ruth 3:3). **ointments:** Perfumes (Esther 2:12). • The Church, when she makes use of the bath, must be accompanied by two maids. For by faith in Christ and a love for God she confesses and receives the laver of Baptism. And what is the oil she requests but the Holy Spirit with which believers are anointed (see St. Hippolytus, *Commentary on Daniel* 1, 16).

13:21 was with you: A euphemism for sexual intimacy. According to the Mosaic Law, this would make Susanna an adulteress subject to the death penalty (Lev 20:10; Deut 22:22).

13:22 I shall not escape: In biblical times, the testimony of one woman would never prevail over the corroborating testimony of two men.

---

*13:1: The story of Susanna, here translated from the Greek of Theodotion, is accepted by the Catholic Church as canonical Scripture and placed among the deuterocanonical writings. It is prefixed to the book of Daniel in the Septuagint Greek, but in the Vulgate Latin it is placed here as chapter 13.

your hands. [23]I choose not to do it and to fall into your hands, rather than to sin in the sight of the Lord."

24 Then Susanna cried out with a loud voice, and the two elders shouted against her. [25]And one of them ran and opened the garden doors. [26]When the household servants heard the shouting in the garden, they rushed in at the side door to see what had happened to her. [27]And when the elders told their tale, the servants were greatly ashamed, for nothing like this had ever been said about Susanna.

The Elders Testify against Susanna

28 The next day, when the people gathered at the house of her husband Jo'akim, the two elders came, full of their wicked plot to have Susanna put to death. [29]They said before the people, "Send for Susanna, the daughter of Hilki'ah, who is the wife of Jo'akim." [30]So they sent for her. And she came, with her parents, her children, and all her kindred.

31 Now Susanna was a woman of great refinement, and beautiful in appearance. [32]As she was veiled, the wicked men ordered her to be unveiled, that they might feed upon her beauty. [33]But her family and friends and all who saw her wept.

34 Then the two elders stood up in the midst of the people, and laid their hands upon her head. [35]And she, weeping, looked up toward heaven, for her heart trusted in the Lord. [36]The elders said, "As we were walking in the garden alone, this woman came in with two maids, shut the garden doors, and dismissed the maids. [37]Then a young man, who had been hidden, came to her and lay with her. [38]We were in a corner of the garden, and when we saw this wickedness we ran to them. [39]We saw them embracing, but we could not hold the man, for he was too strong for us, and he opened the doors and dashed out. [40]So we seized this woman and asked her who the young man was, but she would not tell us. These things we testify."

41 The assembly believed them, because they were elders of the people and judges; and they condemned her to death.

42 Then Susanna cried out with a loud voice, and said, "O eternal God, who discern what is secret, who are aware of all things before they come to be, [43]you know that these men have borne false witness against me. And now I am to die! Yet I have done none of the things that they have wickedly invented against me!"

Daniel Rescues Susanna

44 The Lord heard her cry. [45]And as she was being led away to be put to death, God aroused the holy spirit of a young lad named Daniel; [46]and he cried with a loud voice, "I am innocent of the blood of this woman."

47 All the people turned to him, and said, "What is this that you have said?" [48]Taking his stand in the midst of them, he said, "Are you such fools, you sons of Israel? Have you condemned a daughter of Israel without examination and without learning the facts? [49]Return to the place of judgment. For these men have borne false witness against her."

50 Then all the people returned in haste. And the elders said to him, "Come, sit among us and inform us, for God has given you that right." [51]And Daniel said to them, "Separate them far from each other, and I will examine them."

52 When they were separated from each other, he summoned one of them and said to him, "You old relic of wicked days, your sins have now come home, which you have committed in the past, [53]pronouncing unjust judgments, condemning the innocent and letting the guilty go free, though the Lord said, 'Do not put to death an innocent and righteous person.' [54]Now then, if you really saw her, tell me this: Under what tree did you see them being intimate with each other?" He answered, "Under a mastic tree."[a] [55]And Daniel said, "Very well! You have lied against your own head, for the angel of God has received the sentence from God and will immediately cut[a] you in two."

56 Then he put him aside, and commanded them to bring the other. And he said to him, "You offspring of Canaan and not of Judah, beauty has

---

13:23 I choose not: Death and disgrace are chosen over disobedience to the Lord. Susanna's determination to avoid sexual sin is reminiscent of Joseph's commitment to chastity in Genesis (Gen 39:7–9) (CCC 2337). • God permitted the dispute in order to make known the chastity of Susanna. She endured an intense struggle, more intense than that of the patriarch Joseph. For he, a man, contended against one woman; but Susanna, a woman, contended against two men and was made a spectacle before men and angels. Even so, nothing could shake her fortitude (St. John Chrysostom, *Sermon on Susanna*).

13:25 opened the garden doors: A setup to make it look as though someone had fled the scene (13:39).

13:32 she was veiled: A sign of feminine modesty (Gen 24:65) (CCC 2521–22).

13:34 laid their hands: A formal prelude to the execution of a criminal by stoning (Lev 24:14).

13:45 Daniel: Moved by God to intervene as a legal advocate for Susanna. First, he protests that judicial protocol has not been followed, for the accusers have not been cross-examined to ensure the reliability of their testimony (13:48). Then he proceeds to expose the plot by getting the accusers to incriminate themselves as false witnesses (13:52–61).

13:52–59 Daniel's interrogation of the elders. He ingeniously reveals a discrepancy in their testimony about the location of the alleged crime. A double word-play appears in the Greek text: the term for "mastic tree" (*schinos*) resembles the verb "cut" (*schizō*), and the term for "oak" (*prinos*) resembles the verb "saw" (*prizō*). • Susanna is a type of the Church, and her husband Joakim is a type of Christ. The two elders prefigure those who plot against the Church and judge the righteous unjustly. They strive to afflict the Church, intending to corrupt her, yet they do not agree with each other (St. Hippolytus, *Commentary on Daniel* 1, 14).

13:56 offspring of Canaan: The Canaanites were infamous for their sexual depravity (Lev 18:1–30).

---

[a] The Greek words for *mastic tree* and *cut* are so similar that the use of *cut* is ironic wordplay.

deceived you and lust has perverted your heart. [57]This is how you both have been dealing with the daughters of Israel, and they were intimate with you through fear; but a daughter of Judah would not endure your wickedness. [58]Now then, tell me: Under what tree did you catch them being intimate with each other?" He answered, "Under an evergreen oak."[b] [59]And Daniel said to him, "Very well! You also have lied against your own head, for the angel of God is waiting with his sword to saw[b] you in two, that he may destroy you both."

[60] Then all the assembly shouted loudly and blessed God, who saves those who hope in him. [61]And they rose against the two elders, for out of their own mouths Daniel had convicted them of bearing false witness; [62]and they did to them as they had wickedly planned to do to their neighbor; acting in accordance with the law of Moses, they put them to death. Thus innocent blood was saved that day.

[63] And Hilki′ah and his wife praised God for their daughter Susanna, and so did Jo′akim her husband and all her kindred, because nothing shameful was found in her. [64]And from that day onward Daniel had a great reputation among the people.

Daniel and the Priests of Bel

14 [*]When King Asty′ages was laid with his fathers, Cyrus the Persian received his kingdom. [2]And Daniel was a companion of the king, and was the most honored of his friends.

[3] Now the Babylonians had an idol called Bel, and every day they spent on it twelve busels of fine flour and forty sheep and fifty gallons of wine. [4]The king revered it and went every day to worship it. But Daniel worshiped his own God.

[5] And the king said to him, "Why do you not worship Bel?" He answered, "Because I do not revere man-made idols, but the living God, who created heaven and earth and has dominion over all flesh."

[6] The king said to him, "Do you not think that Bel is a living God? Do you not see how much he eats and drinks every day?" [7]Then Daniel laughed, and said, "Do not be deceived, O king; for this is but clay inside and brass outside, and it never ate or drank anything."

[8] Then the king was angry, and he called his priests and said to them, "If you do not tell me who is eating these provisions, you shall die. [9]But if you prove that Bel is eating them, Daniel shall die, because he blasphemed against Bel." And Daniel said to the king, "Let it be done as you have said."

[10] Now there were seventy priests of Bel, besides their wives and children. And the king went with Daniel into the temple of Bel. [11]And the priests of Bel said, "Behold, we are going outside; you yourself, O king, shall set forth the food and mix and place the wine, and shut the door and seal it with your signet. [12]And when you return in the morning, if you do not find that Bel has eaten it all, we will die; or else Daniel will, who is telling lies about us." [13]They were unconcerned, for beneath the table they had made a hidden entrance, through which they used to go in regularly and consume the provisions. [14]When they had gone out, the king set forth the food for Bel. Then Daniel ordered his servants to bring ashes and they sifted them throughout the whole temple in the presence of the king alone. Then they went out, shut the door and sealed it with the king's signet, and departed. [15]In the night the priests came with their wives and children, as they were accustomed to do, and ate and drank everything.

[16] Early in the morning the king rose and came, and Daniel with him. [17]And the king said, "Are the seals unbroken, Daniel?" He answered, "They are unbroken, O king." [18]As soon as the doors were opened, the king looked at the table, and shouted

---

13:57 intimate ... through fear: Unbeknownst to the Jewish community, the elders have more than once been successful in getting sex by intimidation. However, their criminal past cannot be concealed from God, who discerns "what is secret" (13:42).

13:62 law of Moses: Requires that false witnesses receive the very punishment they have intended for the falsely accused (Deut 19:16–19).

14:1–42 The twin stories of Bel (14:1–22) and the Dragon (14:23–42). In both, Daniel uses clever tactics to expose the folly of idolatry against the claims of their pagan devotees. At issue is whether the deities of Babylon are actually *living* gods. From Daniel's Jewish perspective, this is not only naïve but laughable (14:7, 19). The God of Israel is the only living and true God worthy of the name (14:5, 25, 41) (CCC 2112).

14:1 Astyages: The last king of Media, who ruled from 585 until 550 B.C., when Cyrus II of Persia overthrew the Medes and incorporated their realm into his own.

14:2 friends: A title given to the king's trusted advisors (1 Kings 4:5). In one Greek version of this passage (LXX, but not Θ), Daniel is identified as a "priest". Although it is true that "Daniel" is a Levitical family name (Ezra 8:2), it is also a Davidic family name (1 Chron 3:1). Other ancient traditions thus describe Daniel, not as a Levitical priest, but as a descendant of the tribe of Judah (*Lives of the Prophets* 4, 1) and a member of the royal house of David (Josephus, *Antiquities* 10, 186–88).

14:3 Bel: Another name for Marduk, the chief deity in the Babylonian pantheon (Is 46:1; Jer 50:2; 51:44). Non-biblical sources confirm that Marduk was fed vast quantities of food on a daily basis.

14:5 man-made: A standard Jewish critique of idolatry, insisting that idols are nothing more than lifeless images manufactured by human craftsmen (Ps 115:4–8; Is 44:9–20; Jer 10:3–9; Hab 2:18–19).

14:11 seal it: For the meaning of this, see note on 6:17.

14:13 hidden entrance: The cult of Bel and his food consumption is a sham, kept secret by priests with a vested interest in feeding their families with the offerings of the people.

14:14 ashes: Undetectable during the night (14:15).

---

[b] The Greek words for *evergreen oak* and *saw* are so similar that the use of *saw* is ironic wordplay.

[*] 14:1: Bel and the Dragon. These stories, here translated from the Greek of Theodotion, are added at the end of Daniel by both Greek and Vulgate. The latter treats the appendix as chapter 14, but attaches verse 1 to the preceding chapter as 13:65.

in a loud voice, "You are great, O Bel; and with you there is no deceit, none at all."

19 Then Daniel laughed, and restrained the king from going in, and said, "Look at the floor, and notice whose footsteps these are." ²⁰The king said, "I see the footsteps of men and women and children."

21 Then the king was enraged, and he seized the priests and their wives and children; and they showed him the secret doors through which they were accustomed to enter and devour what was on the table. ²²Therefore the king put them to death, and gave Bel over to Daniel, who destroyed it and its temple.

Daniel Kills a Dragon

23 There was also a great dragon, which the Babylonians revered. ²⁴And the king said to Daniel, "You cannot deny that this is a living god; so worship him." ²⁵Daniel said, "I will worship the Lord my God, for he is the living God. ²⁶But if you, O king, will give me permission, I will slay the dragon without sword or club." The king said, "I give you permission."

27 Then Daniel took pitch, fat, and hair, and boiled them together and made cakes, which he fed to the dragon. The dragon ate them, and burst open. And Daniel said, "See what you have been worshiping!"

28 When the Babylonians heard it, they were very indignant and conspired against the king, saying, "The king has become a Jew; he has destroyed Bel, and slain the dragon, and slaughtered the priests." ²⁹Going to the king, they said, "Hand Daniel over to us, or else we will kill you and your household." ³⁰The king saw that they were pressing him hard, and under compulsion he handed Daniel over to them.

Daniel in the Lions' Den

31 They threw Daniel into the lions' den, and he was there for six days. ³²There were seven lions in the den, and every day they had been given two human bodies and two sheep; but these were not given to them now, so that they might devour Daniel.

33 Now the prophet Habak'kuk was in Jude'a. He had boiled pottage and had broken bread into a bowl, and was going into the field to take it to the reapers. ³⁴But the angel of the Lord said to Habak'kuk, "Take the dinner which you have to Babylon, to Daniel, in the lions' den." ³⁵Habak'kuk said, "Sir, I have never seen Babylon, and I know nothing about the den." ³⁶Then the angel of the Lord took him by the crown of his head, and lifted him by his hair and set him down in Babylon, right over the den, with the rushing sound of the wind itself.

37 Then Habak'kuk shouted, "Daniel, Daniel! Take the dinner which God has sent you." ³⁸And Daniel said, "You have remembered me, O God, and have not forsaken those who love you." ³⁹So Daniel arose and ate. And the angel of God immediately returned Habak'kuk to his own place.

40 On the seventh day the king came to mourn for Daniel. When he came to the den he looked in, and there sat Daniel. ⁴¹And the king shouted with a loud voice, "You are great, O Lord God of Daniel, and there is no other besides you." ⁴²And he pulled Daniel[a] out, and threw into the den the men who had attempted his destruction, and they were devoured immediately before his eyes.

14:22 put them to death: As stipulated in 14:8.

14:23 great dragon: Presumably a crocodile or large snake. The veneration of such a reptile in Babylon is so far unknown from other ancient sources.

14:27 pitch, fat, and hair: Once ingested, the concoction distends the reptile's stomach until it bursts open, resulting in death. The dragon is thus exposed as a mortal animal rather than a "living god" (14:24).

14:31–42 Daniel is again condemned to the lions' den. As in the first episode in 6:10–28, he is taken up unharmed, only to see his opponents hurled into the pit and devoured instantly.

14:31 six days: Explains the need for Daniel to eat (14:34).

14:32 seven lions: Accustomed to feeding on the flesh of 24 carcasses over a six-day period.

14:33 Habakkuk: The prophet who foretold the Babylonian conquest of Judah and Jerusalem in the sixth century B.C. His oracles are preserved in the Book of Habakkuk, which stands among the Minor Prophets in the OT.

14:36 by his hair: Recalls how an angel gave the prophet Ezekiel mystical transport by grasping a lock of his hair (Ezek 8:3).

14:41 You are great, O Lord: The king had previously said, "You are great, O Bel" (14:18). The confession comes after witnessing the rescue of Daniel and having his eyes opened to the foolishness of idolatry. Similar responses were given by Kings Nebuchadnezzar (2:47) and Darius (6:26–27) after seeing the power of God at work in Daniel's life. **there is no other:** An assertion of monotheism, the biblical belief that Yahweh is the only true God (Deut 4:39; 32:39; Is 45:5) (CCC 200–202).

[a] Gk *him*.

Study Questions

Chapter 1

For understanding
1. **1:1.** What are the two different systems of counting a king's reign that were used in the Near East, and for what disparity would they provide a plausible resolution? Why would Nebuchadnezzar wish to make a show of force in Jerusalem following his victory over Egypt in 605 B.C.? When did Jehoiakim and Nebuchadnezzar reign? What other incursions into Judea by Nebuchadnezzar does the Bible mention?
2. **1:2.** What does Nebuchadnezzar plunder from the Temple, and where was it taken? What theme does the transfer of vessels from one temple to another introduce?
3. **1:7.** What kinds of names do Daniel and his friends have? What kinds of names mark them as servants of Nebuchadnezzar?
4. **1:8.** Why did Daniel avoid the king's food? What are some possible factors behind his decision? Of what was abstinence from Gentile foods a hallmark in biblical times?

For application
1. **1:7.** What does your given name mean to you? Why does the Church encourage the taking of a saint's name at Confirmation? Why did you select your patron saint, and what does the name of that saint mean to you now?
2. **1:8, 12.** Why do some people choose to become vegetarians? How might their motives compare or contrast with Daniel's?
3. **1:17.** What is the difference between the learning and wisdom you acquire by your own efforts and the wisdom that God gives? What characterizes his wisdom? As you examine your own relationship with God, do you see any change in your learning and wisdom regarding him?
4. **1:18–20.** What kind of wisdom and understanding do you think Nebuchadnezzar was probably looking for in the young men? If someone were to examine you on your understanding of religious matters, what would he find?

Chapter 2

For understanding
1. **2:1–49.** How does historical evidence confirm the way Daniel begins his career as a renowned wise man and courtier? What story does his rise to the royal court in Babylon recall? What similarities exist in the two cases?
2. **2:2.** What is the original meaning of the term *Chaldeans*, and where in Daniel does it appear to be used that way? What is it used more narrowly to mean here? According to Herodotus, who were Chaldean sages?
3. **2:18. Word Study: Mystery.** What does the Persian loanword *raz* mean? In its nine appearances in the Book of Daniel, to what does the mystery refer? For what will the association forged between "mystery" and "kingdom" in Daniel become the backdrop? What suggests that Paul probably has this association in mind? Where does the Aramaic word *raz* appear outside the Bible, and to what does it refer?
4. **2:31–45.** As an allegory of political history in the ancient Near East, what do the four metals and their sequence in Nebuchadnezzar's dream represent? What will happen in the days of the fourth empire? Theologically, what does the dream reveal? To what might the smashing of the image refer?
5. **2:35.** What does the great mountain represent? What significance do mountains have in the biblical world? What implied contrast may one detect here? How does the expanding mountain in Daniel recall the exaltation of Mount Zion?

For application
1. **2:1.** Describe a dream that troubled you for some time afterward. What bothered you about it? In general, what importance do you attach to dreams, especially troubling or recurring dreams?
2. **2:20–23.** How does Daniel go about blessing God in this prayer? What is his focus of attention? How might this approach help you in your own prayer?
3. **2:28.** God sometimes reveals to us mysteries about our own behavior; for example, about why one's relationship with him seems to have stalled. Have you ever prayed for understanding about a problem and received insight as a result? How did the insight affect the resolution of the problem?
4. **2:31–45.** Read the note for these verses. What do you believe about God's control over human history at large? What about his control over the political, economic, and military issues of today? How does your belief affect your confidence in God's provision for you and your loved ones in times of stress?

Chapter 3

For understanding
1. **Topical Essay: The Four Kingdoms in Daniel.** If the rise and fall of foreign states would not normally have interested Daniel's readers, what did? How do modern exegetes identify the four kingdoms, and what problems does their interpretation encounter? Why is the traditional reading more convincing?
2. **3:5.** What does the presence of three musical instruments with Greek names have to do with the dating of the Book of Daniel? What does mandatory prostration before an image signify to the Babylonians?
3. *3:1–68* (italics). What are the two poems that stand between 3:23 and 3:24 of the Hebrew-Aramaic text of Daniel? What does the Catholic Church consider these deuterocanonical portions of Daniel to be?
4. *3:3–22* (italics). What kind of prayer is Azariah's prayer, and what does it acknowledge? Why are the three youths facing persecution and death in spite of their heroic faithfulness? Where do similar confessions appear in the Bible?

5. **3:25.** What is burned off of the three young men in the furnace, and what remains unharmed? Who is the fourth figure sighted in the flames? According to St. Jerome, whom does this angel foreshadow?

For application
1. **3:16–18.** If the government were to pass a law requiring all citizens either to violate one of the Ten Commandments or to support that violation under pain of severe penalties (such as heavy fines or confiscation of property), what would you do? How important is your Christian witness in such circumstances?
2. **3:1–22 (italics).** In these verses, Azariah expresses contrition, not for his own sins, but for the sins of the people to whom he belongs. If one is not personally responsible for the sins of his culture, why make such a prayer? What spiritual benefits might one realize from such a confession? Why is prayer for your country valuable?
3. **3:28–68 (italics).** In their song, the three young men praise God for his goodness and then call on all creation (including themselves) to praise him; note the same pattern of prayer in Ps 148. Given their circumstances, what good is their praise? What effects might praise have on one's attitude toward prayer, regardless of the circumstances?
4. **3:26 (italics), 3:25 (normal font).** Read CCC 334–36 on angels in the life of the Church. Do you share the Church's belief in guardian angels? Have you ever sought the intercession of your guardian angel? If not, what prevents you from doing so?

Chapter 4

For understanding
1. **4:8.** What does the name Belteshazzar mean? Which Babylonian god had the title Bel? What do Nebuchadnezzar's words recall?
2. **4:10–18.** As a parable of judgment, about what does Nebuchadnezzar's dream warn him? What does the banded stump signify? What has archaeology discovered with respect to Nebuchadnezzar?
3. **4:25.** How does modern psychiatry define Nebuchadnezzar's mental illness? What can one make of the seven years (or months) of his insanity? What does Josephus, the Jewish historian, report in this connection?
4. **4:27.** What early Jewish belief does Daniel's advice express? How would the sinful Nebuchadnezzar pay down his debt to God? What are the benefits of almsgiving?

For application
1. **4:2.** What "signs and wonders" has God wrought in your life? With whom have you shared them? What is the difference between *boasting* about what has happened and *giving testimony* to it? According to 2 Cor 12:9, about what should you boast?
2. **4:3.** Read CCC 541–42. How do Christians understand the "everlasting kingdom" to which Nebuchadnezzar refers? How would you describe your own place in it?
3. **4:8–9.** What kind of person should you consult for spiritual advice? When a person such as a confessor or spiritual director gives you advice or an admonition, do you have a duty to follow it?
4. **4:33.** Have you ever had experience with mental illness, either in yourself or in a loved one? How have you dealt with it? Has it challenged your faith and your hope in God?
5. **4:34.** Although prayer may not result in a miraculous healing of mental or emotional problems, what benefit might prayer—especially prayer of praise—provide for problems such as depression, anxiety, or irrational fears?

Chapter 5

For understanding
1. **5:1.** What does the name Belshazzar mean? Strictly speaking, what position did Belshazzar occupy? Why did Belshazzar exercise royal authority? Why could he only offer to make the interpreter of the writing the "third ruler" in the kingdom?
2. **5:22–23.** Of what four things is Belshazzar guilty?
3. **5:25.** To what does the cryptic message on the wall relate? To what does the language of commercial transaction point? How does Daniel reinforce this message of judgment?
4. **5:28.** Who were the Medes and the Persians?
5. **5:31.** What does history know of Darius the Mede? What has modern scholarship often declared him to be? What three attempts have scholars who accept the historicity of Daniel made to identify Darius the Mede?

For application
1. **5:2–4.** What were you taught about handling vessels used to celebrate the Holy Sacrifice of the Mass? Why are such vessels not to be used as ordinary dinner vessels are used? Why does CCC 2120 describe sacrilege as a "grave sin"?
2. **5:10–12.** Read the note for verse 10. How does the role of the queen in this passage resemble that of the Mother of Jesus? What does Mary do for us in regard to her Son?
3. **5:20–22.** Why is the virtue of humility important in one's relationship with God? How can *humiliation* be considered a blessing? As illustrated by Belshazzar's attitude, what happens when one refuses to learn from humiliation?
4. **5:27.** This verse has become something of a proverb. On what "balances" is Belshazzar being weighed? Who weighs your own spiritual state, and how might knowing that be an incentive toward growth?

Chapter 6

For understanding
1. **6:1–28.** What story elements of chap. 3 does this court tale in chap. 6 (about Daniel's rescue from the lions' den) mirror?
2. **6:1.** What are satraps? What does the reference to 120 satraps probably include?

3. **6:7.** What was the layout of the den of lions? Why did the Persians not use fire to execute criminals, as the Babylonians did? What may the change in methods of capital punishment from Babylonian to Persian times indicate?
4. **6:10.** Why did Daniel go to pray in his house? According to St. Jerome, what do we learn from this passage? What inspired the practice of praying toward Jerusalem?

For application
1. **6:3–4a.** According to CCC 2539–40, why is envy a capital—and, in some cases, a mortal—sin? Why does St. Augustine call envy diabolical? Have you ever struggled with envy?
2. **6:10.** What kind of prayer does Daniel make in his room, even though he knows his life is in danger? What lesson about our own prayer can we derive from Daniel's approach to prayer?
3. **6:10.** What is the significance of the fact that Daniel prays facing Jerusalem? Why does Catholic liturgical tradition recommend celebrating certain sacraments, such as the Eucharist, facing east?
4. **6:14–18.** In these verses, the king realizes that he has done something that cannot be undone, the lethal consequences of which he did not intend and could not avert. Does his mistake resemble incidents from your own life? How can mistakes like these assist your growth in both wisdom and charity?

Chapter 7

For understanding
1. **7:2–8.** What do the four beasts in Daniel's dream parallel? What do both sets of images represent? What does each beast represent? What do the zoological images symbolize?
2. **7:8.** How has the "little horn" in this verse been identified by different interpreters? Where else in Scripture have clues been found to link him with a historical figure?
3. **7:13.** With what are the "clouds of heaven" associated in the biblical world? Although the expression "son of man" normally refers to a mortal human being, what function does the term serve here? With whom do some identify the Danielic "son of man"? More likely, what is he? In the Gospels, when does Jesus adopt the messianic interpretation? According to Justin Martyr, what do the words "like a son of man" show? How does St. Jerome interpret this figure in his *Commentary on Daniel*?
4. **7:25.** How long a period is the "time, two times, and half a time" in this passage? In the Book of Revelation, what happens in this period of time? How does that match what happened historically in the Jewish revolt that sparked the Roman conquest of Jerusalem?

For application
1. **7:9–10.** Why do many of the visions of God in Scripture include images of fire? Aside from fire as an image of punishment, what other things does fire do or stand for that might be associated with God and his work? (Hint: How is fire associated with emotions, metallurgy, and even medicine?)
2. **7:13.** Read the part of the note for this verse about the association of clouds with divinity. What do clouds represent in that context? Why, as at the Transfiguration, would the apostles be afraid when a cloud surrounds them?
3. **7:15–16.** Daniel wants to understand his visions of the future. How much of the future do you think it advisable to know? For what purpose? If these visions are not merely to satisfy curiosity, what purpose do they serve?
4. **7:21–22.** In Scripture, the *horn* is often a symbol of strength and sometimes refers to forces of persecution. How are such forces arrayed against the Church in our day? What does Scripture, both here and in the Book of Revelation, indicate will happen to these horns? How might that apply to modern forces of persecution?

Chapter 8

For understanding
1. **8:2–14.** With what is Daniel's second vision concerned? To whom do the goat's "conspicuous horn" and the "four conspicuous horns" refer? Who is the "little horn"?
2. **8:11.** Who is the "Prince of the host"? To what does the "continual burnt offering" refer? What did Antiochus IV do to the Jerusalem Temple?
3. **8:14.** How long a time is 2,300 evenings and mornings, and to what does the sum possibly refer? Who restored the Temple after that time?
4. **8:25.** What title did the Seleucid king Antiochus IV give himself? How was he brought low "by no human hand"?

For application
1. **8:10.** Read the commentary on this verse. What is the strategy behind a persecutor eliminating the "wise among God's people" when he first takes power? In modern history, can you think of examples where that has happened? What happened to God's people as a result?
2. **8:17.** Why do you think the appearance of an angel inspires such fear in humans? How does the priest Zachariah's response to Gabriel's appearance in Luke 1:12 contrast with Mary's in 1:29?
3. **8:23.** What character trait is the expression "a king of bold countenance" intended to describe? What might a "bold countenance" look like in people you know? What attitude does it suggest toward God?

Chapter 9

For understanding
1. **9:2.** To what prophecy of Jeremiah does Daniel refer regarding Judah? How many years actually elapsed before the captives were allowed to return to their homeland?

2. **9:21.** Who is "the man Gabriel"? What is the time of the evening sacrifice, and why does the prophet allude to it at a time when no sacrifices would have been offered in the Temple? How does the appearance of Gabriel to Daniel parallel his appearance to Zechariah, father of John the Baptist?

3. **9:24–27.** What is the meaning of Daniel's prophecy of the 70 weeks? Into what three categories can most interpretations of this oracle be fitted?

4. **9:24.** What are the "seventy weeks of years", and what do they have to do with the penitential period that Israel must undergo? For what was this new revelation to Daniel designed to prepare the Jewish exiles? How does multiplying the time of exile by seven have its explanation in Leviticus and the Jubilee cycles? What parallels are noticeable between Daniel 9 and Isaiah 53?

5. **9:24. Word Study: Weeks.** How is *shabua'* used in Daniel 9:24, and to what does it refer? How long a time does the prophecy cover? What biblical precedents are there for equating one day with one year?

6. **9:25.** To what do the terms "restore" and "build" refer? Historically, how are they related to the joint mission of Ezra and Nehemiah? In light of this, with what is the "going forth of the word" best identified? Over what period, then, does the 70th week of the prophecy extend? To whom does the "anointed one" refer?

7. **9:27.** To what does the "strong covenant" seemingly refer? How is the cessation of sacrifice and offerings best understood in connection with the sacrifice of Christ? What is the "wing of abominations"?

For application

1. **9:3.** Christians are encouraged to seek God through fasting and acts of mortification, as Daniel does in this verse. How do these activities contribute to a healthy prayer life? What part do they play in your own prayer life?

2. **9:8.** How many meanings for the word "face" can you think of? What does the expression "confusion of face" mean? If you are a parent, how might it describe the appearance of a child whom you catch in the act of wrongdoing?

3. **9:17.** Why does Daniel pray for the restoration of the sanctuary in Jerusalem "for your own sake, O Lord"? In other words, how is God's reputation related to the restoration of the Temple? How might such a motive (i.e., for God's own sake) apply to your prayer as you pray for the Church?

4. **9:24.** Read CCC 1472 on the consequences of sin and CCC 1030–32 on Purgatory. How does Gabriel's announcement of the "seventy weeks of years" remind you of the doctrine of Purgatory? Why is Purgatory necessary for some people? How should one live so as to avoid the need for Purgatory?

Chapter 10

For understanding

1. **10:1—12:13.** What is the focus of Daniel's fourth and final vision?

2. **10:13.** What does the term "prince" designate in this passage? What is the Jewish belief behind this, and from where does it come? How does St. Thomas Aquinas explain the "opposition" between angels? Who is Michael, and what does he do? What other angels are identified by name in the Bible?

3. **10:20.** What is the significance of Persia and Greece in this passage? How long did their domination last?

For application

1. **10:2–3.** Given the context of the previous chapter, why is Daniel mourning for three weeks? Why is it proper to call at least the first three weeks of Lent a period of mourning—and for what? What penitential practices do you observe during Lent?

2. **10:12.** What does it mean to humble oneself in prayer? According to CCC 2559, how does one practice humility in prayer? Does your own prayer reflect that humility?

3. **10:16–17.** Have you ever questioned whether your prayers of intercession are effective? Since intercession "is a prayer of petition which leads us to pray as Jesus did" (CCC 2634), what examples can you find in Scripture where Jesus prays for others? What can you learn from these examples? Why is it *necessary* for you to pray for others?

4. **10:18.** Why would strength and courage be necessary for one who intercedes in prayer? What is there about prayer that might call for courage?

Chapter 11

For understanding

1. **11:5–20.** What long-standing conflict do these verses envision? Since Israel is the geographical center of the prophecy, which monarchs are the "king of the north" and the "king of the south"?

2. **11:21–45.** Whose reign do these verses describe? How does history remember him? How has Christian tradition often viewed him, and why?

3. **11:30.** To whom does the Hebrew name Kittim normally refer, and to whom does it refer here and in the Dead Sea Scrolls? What was Antiochus IV's response to the arrival of the "ships of Kittim"? With whom did he then make alliances?

4. **11:31.** What is the "abomination that makes desolate" (sometimes called the "abomination of desolation")? How long did this abomination last, and who ended it? What recurring pattern does Daniel seem to detect in his typological vision of history? To what did Jesus apply the same language?

For application

1. **11:5–20.** Read the note for these verses. How long has conflict in this area of the world been going on? What are some of the reasons for conflict in this region today? Assuming that some motives for conflict surround a desire for revenge over past misdeeds, what would be necessary in order to bring about peace?

2. **11:31–33.** Reports of the desecration of churches and the martyrdom of Christians surface often in the news these days. Since Jesus promised that persecution would never be far from those who profess his name (e.g., Mt 24:9–22), what should you do to prepare yourself for it?

3. **11:34.** The note for this verse refers to the rebellion of the Maccabees against Antiochus IV Epiphanes. According to CCC 2307–9, what conditions are necessary in order for recourse to military force against an oppressor to be morally legitimate?

Chapter 12

For understanding
1. **12:1.** What "time" is referred to here? What is the "book" mentioned in this verse?
2. **12:2.** For what is sleep a euphemism? How will those who are asleep awake? What is the significance of this passage in the Bible?
3. **12:4.** What function did wax seals serve on rolled-up scrolls? Why is Daniel supposed to seal up the written account of his visions?
4. **12:7.** What is the significance of the man clothed in linen raising his right hand? What is the purpose of the oath? To what do the time, two times, and half a time refer in this context?

For application
1. **12:1.** Like Daniel, the Church regards St. Michael as the archangel who protects God's people from the "wickedness and snares of the devil". What kind of protection do you think God's people most need today? According to Paul's advice in Ephesians 6, how should you prepare yourself for spiritual battle?
2. **12:2.** According to Hebrews 9:27, what happens when you die? What judgment do you expect for yourself, and why? How important is the resurrection of the dead to your faith?
3. **12:8–9.** Recall a time when you prayed for the answer to a problem and were not answered (at least, not directly). What effect did that lack of apparent response have on your faith? How can we learn to grow in trust and hope during difficult times?
4. **12:10.** According to the note for this verse, purification is a spiritual effect of physical martyrdom. How can purification and refinement take place in one's life apart from martyrdom? If Purgatory is a purification after death from the effects of sin (CCC 1031, 1472), is it inevitable?

Chapter 13

For understanding
1. **13:1—14:42.** In what language do chaps. 13 and 14 survive, and in what language were they probably written? What religious traditions exclude these chapters, and what tradition considers them to be fully inspired and canonical Scripture?
2. **13:23.** According to St. John Chrysostom, why did God permit Susanna's dispute with the elders? How was her struggle more intense than that of the patriarch Joseph?
3. **13:45.** How does Daniel, as a legal advocate for Susanna, proceed in her defense?
4. **13:52–59.** What Greek wordplay does Daniel use in his interrogation of the elders? How does St. Hippolytus of Rome interpret this story typologically?

For application
1. **13:7–11.** According to these verses, are the elders engaged in stifling their consciences? What does it take for a person to muffle the voice of his conscience? What obligations does a Christian have regarding his conscience?
2. **13:23.** Which is more valuable to you: your life or the desire to avoid sin? In what sense might death be a better alternative than committing sin (even if one feels forced into it)?
3. **13:27.** According to CCC 2477–79, the elders are guilty of the sin of calumny (among others); but of the sins listed, of which might the servants be guilty in Susanna's regard? How does the Catechism recommend avoiding this sin?
4. **13:44–62.** How does Daniel's defense of Susanna compare with Jesus' defense of the woman taken in adultery (Jn 8:3–11)? In the latter case, how does Jesus' implicit judgment of the elders compare with his judgment of the guilty woman?

Chapter 14

For understanding
1. **14:2.** To whom is the title "friend" given? What type of family name is *Daniel*? While some ancient traditions describe Daniel as a Levite, how do other traditions describe him?
2. **14:3.** For which Babylonian god is Bel another name? What practice do reports from non-biblical sources confirm about Marduk?
3. **14:23.** What kind of reptile is the "great dragon"? What do ancient sources say about the veneration of such a reptile in Babylon?
4. **14:41.** What causes the king to confess the greatness of the one true God? Who else in Daniel make similar responses? What does the king's confession assert?

For application
1. **14:5–7.** How can Christians respect non-Christian religions while holding to the obligation to proclaim the truths of the gospel?
2. **14:10–13.** Read CCC 1584. What happens if a minister does not believe in the effectiveness of the sacrament he is administering but proceeds with the liturgy anyway? If a Christian is baptized, renounces his faith, and later returns to it, why does he not need to be rebaptized?
3. **14:41.** Apart from miracles associated with a person like Daniel, how might one recognize God's power at work in another person's life? What are the fruits of the Spirit, and how do they demonstrate that power? Can your own experience attest to this power in you?

BOOKS OF THE BIBLE

THE OLD TESTAMENT (OT)

Gen	Genesis
Ex	Exodus
Lev	Leviticus
Num	Numbers
Deut	Deuteronomy
Josh	Joshua
Judg	Judges
Ruth	Ruth
1 Sam	1 Samuel
2 Sam	2 Samuel
1 Kings	1 Kings
2 Kings	2 Kings
1 Chron	1 Chronicles
2 Chron	2 Chronicles
Ezra	Ezra
Neh	Nehemiah
Tob	Tobit
Jud	Judith
Esther	Esther
Job	Job
Ps	Psalms
Prov	Proverbs
Eccles	Ecclesiastes
Song	Song of Solomon
Wis	Wisdom
Sir	Sirach (Ecclesiasticus)
Is	Isaiah
Jer	Jeremiah
Lam	Lamentations
Bar	Baruch
Ezek	Ezekiel
Dan	Daniel
Hos	Hosea
Joel	Joel
Amos	Amos
Obad	Obadiah
Jon	Jonah
Mic	Micah
Nahum	Nahum
Hab	Habakkuk
Zeph	Zephaniah
Hag	Haggai
Zech	Zechariah
Mal	Malachi
1 Mac	1 Maccabees
2 Mac	2 Maccabees

THE NEW TESTAMENT (NT)

Mt	Matthew
Mk	Mark
Lk	Luke
Jn	John
Acts	Acts of the Apostles
Rom	Romans
1 Cor	1 Corinthians
2 Cor	2 Corinthians
Gal	Galatians
Eph	Ephesians
Phil	Philippians
Col	Colossians
1 Thess	1 Thessalonians
2 Thess	2 Thessalonians
1 Tim	1 Timothy
2 Tim	2 Timothy
Tit	Titus
Philem	Philemon
Heb	Hebrews
Jas	James
1 Pet	1 Peter
2 Pet	2 Peter
1 Jn	1 John
2 Jn	2 John
3 Jn	3 John
Jude	Jude
Rev	Revelation (Apocalypse)